# The GET-AHEAD COOK

JANE LOVETT

A

**For John and Dad,**
**for everything**

First published in 2018 by Apicius Publishing



ISBN 978-1-911195-63-4

Printed and bound in China by Imago

Project Management by whitefox

# The GET-AHEAD COOK

JANE LOVETT

PHOTOGRAPHY BY TONY BRISCOE

# CONTENTS

# INTRODUCTION

## I love cooking and always have done.

Apart from being naturally greedy myself, I have an instinctive inclination to feed others and this really is one of life's pleasures for me. Indeed, mealtimes form the structure of my day – it's not the afternoon until I've had lunch, however meagre and whatever time that may be. I've always been baffled by people who say they 'forgot to have lunch'. How could they and how do they know when it's the afternoon? Needless to say, the next meal, what it might be and where it's coming from, is never far from my mind.

Of course, I realize this scenario is far from the reality for many people. Inclination, time and ability are just a few of the reasons why cooking becomes a chore and something to resent. All of which is completely understandable. Yet there are many ways of relieving and lessening the daily grind of cooking, as well as the sheer panic frequently induced by even the thought of entertaining.

# GETTING AHEAD



'The secret of getting ahead is getting started.'

MARK TWAIN

**Everyday cooking for loved ones or friends should be a happy experience – food made and served with love, not to mention style and a smile. Planning and preparation, I think, are the key to this, especially for apprehensive cooks or those short of time.**

Getting ahead is fundamental for me. With my organized cap on, I can cope calmly with most things. Without it, I become flappable and stressed, and as far as entertaining is concerned, I don't enjoy a minute of it – the cooking or the assembled company – and far less, clearing up afterwards. Not only does forward preparation reduce stress levels, but it also allows more time to spend with family and friends, as well as eliminating last-minute washing-up considerably. Win, win!

Aside from day-to-day cooking and entertaining, I need to be very organized for the cookery demonstrations I give around the country, not only with the buying of ingredients, but also with the measuring out and careful advance preparation of all the recipes. It is the key to a smoothly run demonstration, which results in a happier, more relaxed me and, consequently, I hope, a better experience for my customers.

It beats me as to why anyone would attempt to simultaneously cook multiple recipes from scratch; yet through my demonstrations I have come to realize that many people believe it's the only option. This is entirely understandable, given that generally recipes reel off the method, with the last instruction being to serve immediately. And so ensues a last-minute frenzy for the cook attempting to get several dishes made from scratch, and finished all at the same time.

Where's the fun in that? We are home cooks first and foremost, and what we bring to the table is far more than just the food. The table is the place where we congregate and come together to communicate, share experiences and delight in the present moment as well as create memories. And so, with a little advance preparation, we might bring more love and joy to the table than pent-up stress. It doesn't even matter if your interpretation of a recipe is different – after all, it's simply about nourishment and conviviality. Cooking is not a competition, so there's no point in getting het up about it. During my days teaching at Leiths School of Food and Wine, it was no surprise that 40 students cooking from exactly the same recipes produced 40 different interpretations, both in taste and presentation. So don't be afraid to put your own stamp on recipes – it might well improve them!

I'm persistently asked how far in advance a recipe can be prepared. The recipes in this book, along with their get-ahead hints, I hope, will go some way to answering this question. They all have get-ahead elements and, be it only a snatched five or ten minutes here or there, even the smallest amount of groundwork eases the task, reaps benefits and makes a difference, especially when taking on several recipes at once.

Cooking should be a joy, so my advice is to prepare ahead as much as time allows and keep it simple. Then enjoy the sense of achievement and pleasure when everything comes together and delight in the happiness it brings.

# ABOUT THE BOOK

## NOTES ON INGREDIENTS

- When I use Rose Harissa paste, Zhoug and tapenade, I like the Belazu brand.
- For a basic curry powder, I suggest Schwartz Medium Curry Powder.
- For prepared ginger in a jar, I like Bart's.
- All dairy products are full-fat.
- All eggs are free-range and large.

**Help is at hand! *The Get-Ahead Cook* is a collection of more than 100 prepare-ahead recipes, achievable for all abilities. Complete with very clear instructions for spreading and, therefore, lightening the load stage by stage, they offer a confidence-boosting guiding hand in the kitchen.**

The original, stylish, contemporary and delicious recipes have been created for day-to-day eating and entertaining, and to inspire the home cook to make food they're proud to serve and that people actually want to eat. They're a natural progression of my easy style – real recipes for the real world, to be produced in real, busy household kitchens where home cooks, both amateur and experienced, are trying to get delicious, fresh, seasonal food onto the table.

I always keep an eye on culinary trends, new ingredients and eating habits. Some of these recipes use slightly more unusual ingredients, with inspiration taken from countries and cultures around the world, but this isn't faddy or gratuitous and I've only included those 'new' ingredients that are easily sourced. An unfamiliar ingredient can be off-putting for a cook unsure of how to deal with it or whether or not it can easily be found, and this book will allay those uncertainties.

That said, the majority of the recipes use straightforward everyday ingredients (and not too many of them) with the emphasis on advance preparation, taste, flavour and presentation. There are lots of useful tips and shortcuts, and the odd cheat here and there, but that doesn't preclude you from making your own pastry, stock and so on, if you prefer. Many of the recipes contain 'don't worry if…' advice, ingredient substitutions and guidance about what to serve with them, which makes some appear longer than they are – so please don't be put off!

We eat with our eyes in the first instance, so presentation is very important, but you won't find any fussy, flashy or 'cheffy' plating-up styles here. I like to encourage imagination in the way food is served – so think outside the box, be inventive and don't necessarily stick to the traditional or the norm; it's quite possible to make the humblest ingredients, or recipe, look fabulous with a little inventiveness and a few good 'props'.

I really hope you will enjoy cooking these recipes, that they will help to make your life a little easier in the kitchen and, better still, propel you out of the kitchen and into the revelry when entertaining. I can wholeheartedly guarantee they work. There is no way I am going to demonstrate a recipe to a room full of people if it's not going to work 100 per cent. They are failsafe and I hope you will be inspired to create and interpret them in your own way.

## OVEN TEMPERATURE CONVERSIONS

| °C | °F | GAS MARK |
|---|---|---|
| 140 | 275 | 1 |
| 150 | 300 | 2 |
| 170 | 325 | 3 |
| 180 | 350 | 4 |
| 190 | 375 | 5 |
| 200 | 400 | 6 |
| 220 | 425 | 7 |
| 230 | 450 | 8 |
| 240 | 475 | 9 |

## MEASURING SPOON CONVERSIONS

| | |
|---|---|
| 1 tablespoon | 15ml |
| ½ tablespoon | 7.5ml |
| 1 teaspoon | 5ml |
| ½ teaspoon | 2.5ml |
| ¼ teaspoon | 1.2ml |
| ⅛ teaspoon | 0.6ml |

## NOTES ON USING THE BOOK

- Read a recipe all the way through fully before embarking on it.
- All temperatures are for conventional electric ovens (see Oven Temperature Conversions, left). For fan-assisted ovens, consult your manual.
- Follow either metric or imperial measurements in a recipe – do not switch between the two.
- Refrigerated food should be brought back to room temperature for at least an hour before cooking. All given oven temperatures and cooking times assume this is the case.
- All spoon measurements are level unless otherwise stated. It is worth investing in a set of accurate measuring spoons (see Measuring Spoon Conversions, left).
- In the absence of fresh stock or pouches of supermarket ready-made stock, use stock cubes. I use 1 cube to 300–425ml (½–¾pt) water.
- Most of the ingredients can be found fairly easily. However, a few might involve a little legwork. Failing that, they can be bought online.
- Everything stored in the fridge should be covered.
- Pregnant or elderly people should avoid food containing raw eggs or unpasteurized cheese.
- Many foods last a lot longer than you might think. Common sense will tell you whether or not something is OK to eat, along with smell and taste, in the time-honoured tradition exercised before the advent of sell-by dates.
- The number of people that some of the recipes will feed depends on whom you are feeding, how many courses you are making and what else is on offer. For example, an older person will eat far less than a ravenous, hollow-legged teenager; people tend to eat less at lunch than at dinner; and, strangely, the larger the number of people, the less they seem to eat.
- Recipes that are suitable for vegetarians are marked with Ⓥ. These exclude meat, poultry, game, fish and shellfish. Some vegetable-based recipes are not marked with Ⓥ because they include cheese that contains, or may contain, animal rennet, but vegetarian cheeses could be substituted if required.

# HINTS & TIPS

### Resting Meat

It is vital to rest meat after cooking; otherwise, all the juices cascade out when it's cut into, leaving it tough and dry. When cooked, remove large joints to a cold plate and leave to stand for 10 minutes to stop the cooking process, then keep warm on the plate, with the oven, warming drawer or cupboard door ajar, for a minimum of 20 minutes; up to an hour is even better and a little bit longer still, is fine. For smaller joints, steaks and poultry breasts, remove to a cold plate for two minutes and then rest for the length of their cooking time. Longer is fine. The meat won't cook any more while resting. If you have been successful, NO juices will seep from the meat when it is cut into!

**There are many tips and shortcuts scattered throughout the book, accompanying the relevant recipes. I hope both those and the ones below will help to put a spring in your culinary step.**

- **Store surplus nuts** in the freezer to prevent them from going rancid. They don't need to be thawed before use in cooking, but it only takes minutes anyway.
- Food processors do not **purée soup** satisfactorily. Use a liquidizer or hand-held wand instead.
- Likewise, a food processor does not work for **chopping onions**, as they will bruise and take on a very unpleasant taste and texture.
- **Eggs** can be boiled and peeled up to 4 days ahead, submerged in cold water, covered and refrigerated.
- Always make sure steam can escape when **keeping any food warm**, by leaving the door or warming drawer ajar. Otherwise, steam builds up, resulting in soggy, discoloured food.
- When **cooking root vegetables**, bring them to the boil in cold salted water. If **boiling green vegetables**, they should be added to boiling salted water then drained when cooked and refreshed by passing them briefly under cold running water, to set the colour and stop them from cooking further. This won't make them go cold.
- Cook **bags of spinach** as soon as they're bought for easier storage. This also means it can be kept longer before eating – the same is true for other fresh vegetables; if they are verging on getting past their best, cook them, store them covered in the fridge and then heat them up when required in a saucepan, oven or microwave.
- The easiest way to **remove the outside ring** from a loose-bottomed tart or springform tin is to stand the tin on top of a mug or bowl; the ring will fall off onto the work surface, preventing burnt (if hot) and dirty arms, and the ring hurtling towards your elbow.
- When **making caramel**, use granulated sugar; being less refined, it dissolves far quicker and more successfully than caster sugar.
- You will **use less oil** if the pan is heated before adding it.
- When **softening onions**, adding a pinch of salt will speed the process up considerably.
- Prolong the life of **fresh herbs** significantly by wrapping them in damp kitchen paper and storing them in a plastic bag or clingfilm in the fridge.
- For a constant supply of **grated Parmesan cheese**, grate a large chunk (or two) using the grater blade of a food processor. Swap for the chopping blade and whizz until fine. Freeze in a bag or container. It doesn't solidify and can be used by the spoonful or scattered as required, straight from the freezer.

# CHOOSING WHAT TO COOK



## A FEW POINTERS ON MENU PLANNING

- Stay within your capabilities.
- Choose recipes according to the time available in the run-up. If time is short, consider serving a few simple canapés instead of a starter, or offer cheese and fruit instead of a pudding. Passing round a box of frozen Maltesers always goes down well, too!
- Choose according to your budget. Seasonal foods will be the best value and at their tastiest.
- Take colour, texture and variety into account, to ensure all the courses are balanced and have contrast.
- Take oven space into consideration.
- Unless you are a proficient cook, plump for a cold starter and pudding, leaving only the main course to cook and thereby cutting the stress by two-thirds.
- Avoid things that require frying at the last minute when entertaining, such as fish fillets. Leave this to professional chefs – it's not conducive to home cooking.
- Nor is assembling intricate stacks of food on individual plates. This is a last-minute task that is stressful when entertaining and almost impossible to do single-handed.
- Avoid the repetition of ingredients, such as fish in the starter and main, or two creamy courses.

**When choosing what to cook, it makes sense to plan according to the time you have available, not just on the day but during the days beforehand, too. We can all get sucked into the optimistic grandiose ideas of cooking a dinner worthy of a *Masterchef* final for our friends and family. But I think it's far better to cook something simple and within one's capabilities well than to be overzealous and end up overstretched, frazzled and unrelaxed as a result. It's really not difficult to make the simplest recipe look utterly delicious and appealing with some imagination and a few good serving dishes. Simple is often best, so be kind to yourself.**

For weekday suppers, a little advance preparation, spread over a few days in the run-up to a particularly busy day or few days, means that good food can be on the table in no time at all, and with minimal effort, at the end of that busy day.

When entertaining, on whatever scale, having at least one course fully prepared in advance is a bonus; two courses are a godsend. I wouldn't dream of choosing more than one recipe that didn't allow at least some advance preparation. There are all sorts of little tricks to employ, too, many of which, in time, become habitual.

Contrary to popular belief, most roasted meat, for example, can be considered 'get-ahead', as it is cooked before guests arrive, affording it a necessary and beneficial resting period, which produces juicier and more tender meat. As long as resting rules are carefully followed (see opposite, far left), not only will the lion's share of your job be done, but also the meat will be greatly improved as a result. The fact that the gravy can then be made and the roasting tin washed up before the first guest arrives is an added bonus.

Making the right choice on the vegetable front can also lighten the last-minute load considerably. Gratins, purées and anything in a sauce are all clever yet delicious ways of avoiding a panic at the eleventh hour. These can be made, mostly, up to a day ahead and, in the case of the first two, completed in their ovenproof serving dishes, ready to be popped into the oven when required – job, and resulting washing-up, done!

Better still, for this purpose, are the recipes that can be made entirely one or two days in advance. Remember that a lot of food tastes better having had a night or two in the fridge, allowing the flavours to meld together, at the same time cutting down on last-minute toil.

There is nothing wrong with a little cheating to help you get ahead, either. There are lots of time-saving ways around some of the more traditional cooking methods (buying, for example, a pre-cooked chicken instead of poaching one; ready-made pastry; ready-made custard for ice creams and soufflés, and so on), so it makes sense to utilize these if needs must.

# SEASONAL MENU PLANS

Some of the recipes in Brunching & Lunching (see page 42) also work well as starters or canapés, and vice versa.

## SPRING

- **Asparagus with Chopped Egg & Anchovy** (left, page 58)
- **Stuffed Shoulder of Lamb with Caper Sauce** (page 132)
- **Rhubarb & Elderflower Fool with Oat Crunch** (page 178)

- **Sizzling Crispy Lamb Salad** (page 60)
- **Monkfish with Peas, Fennel & Romesco Sauce** (page 120)
- **Lime & Coconut Panna Cotta with Mango Purée & Pistachios** (page 162)

## SUMMER

- **Gazpacho with Tapenade Breadsticks** (page 34)
- **Salmon, Courgetti & Asparagus with Lime & Caper Dressing** (left, page 126)
- **Black Cherry, Chocolate & Meringue Ice Cream Cake** (page 176)

- **Crab & Cucumber Mousse** (page 26)
- **Rack of Lamb, Freekeh, Walnuts & Tapenade Crumbs** (page 130)
- **Lemon & Raspberry Shortbread Torte** (page 168)

## AUTUMN

- **Beetroot & Fennel-Cured Salmon** (page 64)
- **Stuffed Pork Fillet with Wild Mushroom Sauce** (left, page 106)
- **Caramelized Apple Creams** (page 169)

- **Chicory, Roquefort & Walnut Salad** (page 38)
- **Duck Confit & Celeriac Purée with Cherry Sauce** (page 110)
- **Pear & Frangipane Tart** (page 184)

## WINTER

- **Tuna & Avocado Ceviche** (page 28)
- **Chicken Legs Baked with Olives & Capers** (left, page 108)
- **Seville Orange Posset with Seville Orange Sablés** (page 179)

- **Potted Prawns** (page 31)
- **Slow-Braised Pork Belly with Sweet Chilli Sauce** (page 115)
- **Hazelnut Meringue & Praline Torte** (page 180)

# CHRISTMAS TIPS



## GET AHEAD FOR THE BIG DAY

**Cooking at Christmas can be a stressful experience. However, I would advise thinking of it as just another Sunday lunch, possibly on a larger scale depending on the number of guests, which is what it boils down to. Lots can be done up to a few months ahead, so whenever you have a spare hour or so in October and November, get cracking. On Christmas Day you'll be very thankful for your foresight, not least because of the reduced amount of washing-up.**

- Cook **chipolata sausages and bacon rolls** and freeze them in the (shallow ovenproof) dish in which they are going to be served, up to 2 months ahead. Thaw the night before and reheat for 10–15 minutes in a hot oven until sizzling. They'll keep warm happily until you need them. Alternatively, complete, as above, up to 3 days in advance.
- **Potatoes for roasting** can be parboiled (for precisely 10 minutes) the day before. Drain and shake in the colander to roughen their edges, then spread out in a roasting tin with a little oil or fat, ready just to pop into the oven the next day. The fat doesn't need to be hot. Or prepare them as above a month or so in advance and freeze. Thaw before cooking.
- Prepare **parsnips** ahead exactly as for roast potatoes, but only parboil for 2 minutes. They, too, can be frozen.
- **Stuffing** can be made up to 2 months in advance and frozen.
- **Bread sauce** can be made up to 3 days in advance and refrigerated, or frozen for 2–3 months. Thaw the day before. It may need a little more milk stirred in.
- **Brandy butter** lasts for 2–3 weeks in the fridge, or can be frozen for 2–3 months.
- Home-made **cranberry sauce** lasts for 2–3 weeks in the fridge, or can be frozen for 2–3 months.
- **Brussels sprouts** can be prepared up to 2 days in advance. I like to halve or quarter them as they cook more evenly and look more appealing and colourful.
- When calculating **cooking times,** remember to factor in at least 30 minutes resting time for the turkey before eating, which can happily, and advisedly, be stretched to an hour or more as long as the bird is kept somewhere warm (see Resting Meat, page 10).
- Make stock for the **gravy** from the turkey (or goose) giblets up to 2 days ahead. Cover them with water, bring to the boil with a quartered onion, bay leaf and any other suitable flavourings you have to hand, and simmer for an hour, before straining and storing in the fridge when cold.
- Always **short of space**, I use the car as an extension of my fridge, especially for a gargantuan turkey – just make sure there's nothing sloppy, that no one drives off with the turkey and that you do your best driving when the car's in larder mode!

# STARTERS & SMALL PLATES

# SESAME PRAWN TOASTS

MAKES APPROXIMATELY 100 TRIANGLES (FEWER IF CUTTING INTO FINGERS)

**1 bunch of spring onions (approximately 9), trimmed**
**1 walnut-sized piece of ginger, peeled and roughly chopped (or 1 tsp ready-prepared from a jar)**
**450g (1lb) raw peeled prawns, dried on kitchen paper**
**1 egg white**
**2 tsp cornflour**
**½ tsp salt**
**12 slices medium-sliced white bread, crusts removed**
**110g (4oz) white sesame seeds (or half white and half black)**
**vegetable oil, for frying**

SERVING SUGGESTIONS

**Sweet chilli, sriracha or dipping sauce, mustard and cress, lime wedges, coriander sprigs**

**A completely make-ahead canapé or starter, which just needs reheating when required. It's always a very popular one, too.**

**1.** Reserve one spring onion for decoration and roughly chop the rest. Process them with the ginger and then add the prawns. Process again until smooth and then add the egg white, cornflour and salt. Process until amalgamated.

**2.** Cut the reserved onion into four halfway along its length, keeping the root and bottom 2.5cm (1in) or so intact. Put into a bowl of cold water in the fridge, where it will curl and fan out within 30 minutes (it will sit there happily for several days).

**3.** Divide the prawn mixture between the 12 slices of bread, spreading it evenly. Spread the sesame seeds out on a small plate (or two plates, if using black seeds as well) and dip the bread, prawn-side down, into them, pressing hard so that they stick to the paste.

**4.** Heat just enough oil to thinly cover the bottom of a frying pan and fry the toasts, prawn-side down, until golden. Turn over and cook the other side until golden, pressing down with a fish slice. You will need to do this in batches, and may need to wipe out the pan with kitchen paper between batches to remove any burnt sesame seeds. Drain on scrunched-up kitchen paper, sprinkle with salt and cut each slice into 8 triangles or fingers.

**5.** Serve warm with the dried fanned-out spring onion and/or any of the suggestions, left.

### Get Ahead

- Make to the end of step 4 up to 2 days in advance, cool and refrigerate, or freeze.
- Reheat in a hot oven for 5–10 minutes (watch them to ensure they don't burn) in one layer on a baking sheet. No need to thaw out first if cooking from frozen, although they will take a little longer.

### Hints & Tips

- Once cut into triangles or fingers, it takes up far less space to store or freeze the toasts in the original square shape of each slice, rather than haphazardly.
- Very good as a starter, cut into fingers and served criss-crossed leaning up against each other, with a blob of chilli sauce, a spring onion, a few salad leaves or any of the serving suggestions, above left.
- I like to serve these piled into Chinese bamboo steaming baskets. Chopsticks add an authentic touch, too.

# SPICY KALE CRISPS



(V)

MAKES 1 MEDIUM BOWL

**200g (7oz) kale leaves, such as curly, purple or cavolo nero**
**olive oil**
**salt**
**chilli flakes or powder (optional)**
**sea salt flakes**

**Utterly delicious, healthy, light as air and very moreish! This can hardly be described as a recipe, but the two important things to heed are to use very, very little oil (hardly any, in fact) and to watch the crisps like a hawk when cooking.**

**1.** Preheat the oven to 180°C. Line a baking sheet with silicone or baking paper.

**2.** If using whole leaves, tear the leaves off the tough spine running through the middle and discard. Tear the leaves into fairly big chunks. Smaller leaves can be left whole. If using pre-sliced/prepared kale from a bag, check it over and remove any tough-looking bits of spine.

**3.** Put into a bowl and add a *very, very small amount* of olive oil – approximately ½ tsp for six large leaves – and massage the oil into the leaves with your fingers, making sure they are all very lightly coated.

**4.** Sprinkle with a little pouring salt and chilli flakes or powder, if using, and spread out on the lined baking sheet in one layer (you may need to cook them in batches).

**5.** Cook in the preheated oven for 10–12 minutes, until crispy but still green – some edges may be a little charred. Watch like a hawk and turn during cooking. The exact time will depend on the chunkiness of the leaves. Remove the smaller, thinner leaves, which will have crisped up first, as soon as they are ready. When cooked and while still hot, scatter over a little sea salt.

**Get Ahead**

The crisps will keep for a week or more in an airtight container or covered bowl. If after this time they go soft, just crisp them up briefly in the oven.

**Hints & Tips**

- A sprinkling of hot smoked paprika, ground cumin or dukkah makes a tasty alternative to chilli.
- Kale crisps are very good on top of fish, eggs and soup, for a final savoury, crunchy and colourful flourish.
- To make 'seaweed', as found in Chinese restaurants, stack up a few leaves, roll tightly into a long cigar shape and slice into very fine strips (chiffonade). Continue as for crisps.

# PORK SCRATCHINGS WITH SPICED APPLE SAUCE

SERVES APPROXIMATELY 8

**225g (8oz) piece of pork skin**
**salt**

**Get Ahead**
They will keep for several days covered, or in an airtight container. Crisp up in a hot oven if necessary. It's best either to hide them or make more than you need!

**Just one word: irresistible! Ask the butcher for a piece of pork skin with a thin layer of fat underneath it. Allow approximately 225g (8oz) for 8 people.**

**1.** Lay the pork skin out flat on a tray, skin-side up, rub with salt and leave uncovered in the fridge for as many days as possible to dry out – one day is fine, two to three even better.

**2.** Preheat the oven to 220°C. Line a baking sheet with foil.

**3.** Dry the skin very well with kitchen paper. Using sharp scissors or a Stanley knife, cut into strips roughly 2cm (¾in) thick and lay skin-side up on the foil.

**4.** Sprinkle with a little more salt and cook at the very top of the oven until golden, crispy and blistered – between 10 and 15 minutes but keep an eye on it. The cooking time will depend on the skin; some takes longer than others.

**5.** Drain on kitchen paper and sprinkle with a tad more salt.

## SPICED APPLE SAUCE

**1 cooking apple, peeled and sliced**
**30g (1oz) caster sugar**
**½ a red chilli, chopped, or chilli flakes**

**1.** Cook the apple with the sugar and a tiny splash of water in a saucepan until soft and fluffy. Taste and add more sugar, if necessary.

**2.** Add chilli a little at a time, to taste.

**Get Ahead**
Make up to 5 days in advance and refrigerate, or freeze.

# ROAST BONE MARROW WITH RED ONION, CAPERS, PARSLEY & GRIDDLED BREAD

SERVES 4

**4 cylinders of beef marrow bone, 5–8cm (2–3in) long, cut from the middle (or 8 cylinders if small)**
**sea salt**
**½ red onion, or a shallot, very thinly sliced or chopped**
**1 small bunch of curly-leaf parsley, roughly chopped**
**1–2 tbsp capers**
**griddled bread (see right), to serve**

### Get Ahead

The uncooked bones freeze beautifully, so it's worth getting a few extra to stash away.

**Bone marrow is surprisingly good for you, containing many important nutrients and fats. It is on the rich side, so serve something light afterwards. At best, it is free from the butcher and at worst, it is inexpensive from a supermarket or a butcher. It's one of my very favourite things!**

**1.** Preheat the oven to 220°C.

**2.** Stand the bones, cut-side up, in a small roasting tin, sprinkle with sea salt and cook at the top of the oven for 20 minutes. Very large bones will take 5 minutes longer.

**3.** Scatter over the onion, parsley and capers, plus a little more sea salt, and serve with griddled bread or toast. Provide some 'prodders' too, for scooping purposes.

## GRIDDLED BREAD

Diagonally slice a rustic-style loaf of bread about 1cm (½in) thick and rub both sides with a little olive oil and some sea salt. Heat a griddle pan until very hot and griddle the bread on both sides until golden and a little charred, with stripes across the middle. Alternatively, slice in half horizontally, griddle the two halves, as above, and then cut into desired shapes. I like to make long thin triangular shapes and serve two of them criss-crossed at the top of each plate.

# BABA GANOUSH WITH TORTILLA CRISPS

(V)

SERVES 4 AS A STARTER (MANY MORE AS A DIP OR PART OF A MEZZE)

**2 large aubergines, very well charred (see below right)**
**2 cloves of garlic, crushed**
**freshly squeezed juice of 1 lemon**
**2 tbsp tahini paste**
**¾ tsp salt**
**1 tbsp olive oil, plus extra for serving**

GARNISH & SERVING SUGGESTIONS

**Olive oil, fresh mint leaves, pomegranate seeds, paprika, cayenne, sumac, smoked sea salt, za'atar, toasted pine nuts, flatbreads, toasted pittas, radishes, vegetable sticks**

### Get Ahead

This will keep happily for 5–6 days, covered, in the fridge.

### Hints & Tips

A little ground cumin is a nice addition, added when processing, as is chopped mint stirred through after processing.

**It's the smoky flavour that makes this so scrumptious, achieved by charring aubergines until their skins are black. A delicious dip, starter or as part of a mezze.**

**1.** Char and cook the aubergines (see below).

**2.** When cool enough to handle, scoop the flesh out into a sieve with a teaspoon. It doesn't matter if a few of the charred black bits get in there – they add more smoky flavour. Gently squeeze/push out some of the excess liquid by pressing the mixture down in the sieve, then transfer to the bowl of a food processor. Add the garlic, lemon juice, tahini paste, salt and olive oil. Whizz until smooth.

**3.** Pile onto a plate or bowl and make a swirly, ridged pattern over the top with a spoon. Trickle with a little olive oil and top with any of the suggestions, below left.

### CHARRING AUBERGINES

**Gas hob:** Preheat the oven to 220°C. Cut off the stalk and, using tongs, hold the aubergine over the flame. Keep turning the aubergine until the skin is charred all over and the middle is beginning to soften – about 5 minutes. Transfer to a baking sheet lined with foil and bake in the preheated oven for 10–15 minutes, or until very soft inside and collapsed.

**Grill or barbecue:** Heat to its highest temperature. Prick the aubergine all over and grill, turning, until the skin is well charred. Finish off in the oven, as above.

**Electric hob:** Heat a griddle pan until very hot. Cut off the stalks and cook, turning, until the aubergine is completely black and falling in on itself.

**Aga:** Cut off the stalk and put the aubergine directly onto the boiling plate. Turn, as each side chars, until completely black and falling in on itself.

## TORTILLA CRISPS

**2–3 large flour tortillas**

**1.** Preheat the oven to 200°C.

**2.** Cut (or snip with scissors) the flour tortillas into chunky triangles, long thin wedges or strips. Bake in the preheated oven in one layer on a baking sheet for 5–8 minutes, or until dried out and semi-crisp. Transfer to a cooling rack. They will crisp up further when cold.

### Get Ahead

Store in an airtight container where they will last for several months.

### Hints & Tips

Any seasonings can be sprinkled over before cooking. Brush the tortillas with olive oil, then dust with your chosen flavouring, such as chilli powder, ground cumin, sumac, smoked paprika or salt.

# LABNEH WITH PITTA CRISPS

(V)

MAKES 16–20 BALLS
SERVES 4–6 AS PART OF A MEZZE

**400g (14oz) full-fat Greek cow's, sheep or goat's milk yoghurt**
**1 tbsp olive oil**
**1 tbsp freshly squeezed lemon juice**
**½ tsp salt**

### Get Ahead

The longer you leave the labneh to drain (see step 2), the thicker it will be. For a soft, velvety texture for dolloping or spreading, leave for 12–24 hours. To make into balls, ideally leave for 48 hours.

### Making labneh balls

Roll into radish-sized balls, put into a sterilized jar and cover with a mix of half and half olive and vegetable oil. Add flavourings of your choice, such as fresh herbs, either on the stem or chopped, bay leaves, lightly crushed coriander or cumin seeds, nigella seeds, chilli flakes, a fresh chilli cut in half, lemon or lime zest, or a mixture of any of the above. The labneh will last 2 weeks or more submerged in the oil and kept in the fridge.

**Cheese doesn't get much easier than this delicious Middle Eastern strained yoghurt. Soft and creamy, it has a wonderful, moreish sour tang and can be enjoyed in thousands of different ways. See below for serving suggestions.**

**1.** Dampen a large piece of muslin (or a coffee filter paper or new J-Cloth) and wring out the excess water. Line a non-reactive sieve with the muslin, leaving the excess hanging over the edges, and sit it over a mixing bowl.

**2.** Mix all the ingredients together and spoon into the sieve. Gather up the overhanging muslin and twist together so the yoghurt forms a ball. Cover with clingfilm and leave for a few hours at room temperature, before refrigerating for 12–24 hours, or longer (see Get Ahead, left).

**3.** Remove the cheese from the muslin. At this stage you might like to stir in any flavouring, such as garlic, spices, freshly chopped herbs, wild garlic, or finely diced vegetables, such as celery, radish or carrot. Or just leave it plain.

### Ideas for serving

- Spread the labneh on a plate in a swirly pattern, dribble over some olive oil and sprinkle with dukkah, sumac, other spices, tapenade or zhoug, as a dip or as part of a mezze.
- Spread toasted sourdough with labneh and top with roast tomatoes and chilli flakes or avocado.
- For sweet labneh, add sugar instead of salt and perhaps a few drops of vanilla extract. Chopped stem ginger stirred in makes a lovely addition. Sprinkle with pistachios and dribble with honey, or enjoy with fresh fruit or a compôte.
- Labneh balls (see far left) can be eaten as they are, or served on cocktail sticks as a canapé. Alternatively, roll them in, or sprinkle them with, flavourings, such as freshly chopped or dried herbs, spices and spice mixes (such as za'atar, dukkah, sumac, smoked paprika, ras el hanout), chilli, nigella seeds, cumin, sesame seeds or chopped pistachios.
- A Kilner jar of labneh balls makes a lovely centrepiece for a board or platter of mixed mezze. Add some olives, tomatoes, radishes, cucumber, asparagus, flatbreads and pitta crisps (see below) and let everyone dig in – enjoy with drinks or as a starter.

## PITTA CRISPS

**pitta breads, wholemeal or plain**

**1.** Cut the pitta breads in half lengthways, and then carefully split open horizontally with a bread knife to produce four long pieces. Snip each piece into 5–7 triangles, producing 20–28 triangles in all, and cook and store in the same way as the Tortilla Crisps (see page 23).

# CRAB & CUCUMBER MOUSSE



SERVES 10–12

**2 cucumbers, unpeeled**
**salt**
**vegetable oil, for greasing**
**280g (10oz) cream cheese, at room temperature**
**2–3 tsp anchovy essence, sauce or paste from a tube**
**300ml (10fl oz) double cream**
**225g (8oz) white crab meat**
**5 leaves of gelatine**
**125ml (4fl oz) fish, chicken or vegetable stock (or ½ a stock cube)**

SERVING SUGGESTIONS

**There are many ways to make this look pretty – thinly sliced half-moons of cucumber arranged overlapping around the top edge, or some sprigs of dill; if set in a ring mould, fill the middle with cooked, peeled prawns, watercress or lightly dressed salad leaves. A few crabs' claws or large shell-on Mediterranean prawns raise this to festive status when arranged imaginatively around the mousse. Nestle in a few lime or lemon wedges, too. Chives, salad cress and edible flowers also look pretty. Melba toast (see Get Ahead, page 31) or Swedish crispbreads make good accompaniments**

**Totally retro and I love it! A light, fresh, very easy and utterly delicious mousse that is good as a starter, for lunch or as part of a buffet. The ideal prepare-ahead starter, this feeds 12 perfectly.**

**1.** Grate the cucumber in a food processor using the grater disc, or the coarse blades of a box grater. Tip into a sieve, sprinkle with a scant teaspoon of salt and leave to drain for a minimum of 30 minutes.

**2.** Lightly grease a 1.2-litre (2-pt) ring mould, tin mould, 10–12 small individual moulds, ramekins or dishes, or one large serving bowl.

**3.** In a large bowl, mix the cream cheese and anchovy essence together, then mix in the cream, half at a time. Squeeze all the excess liquid from the cucumber and stir into the cream mixture with the crab meat.

**4.** Heat the stock to just below boiling point and set aside. Soak the gelatine leaves in a bowl of cold water for 3–5 minutes until softened, then remove, squeeze out the excess water and add the gelatine to the hot (not boiling) stock, stirring it in. Set aside to cool a little.

**5.** Add the warm stock to the crab mixture and mix together well. Don't worry about it being warm. Check the seasoning (the mousse needs to be very well seasoned) and pour into your chosen mould/dishes. Cover and chill, preferably overnight. Turn out (if you wish) and decorate with any of the suggestions (see left).

## Get Ahead

- Make the mousse up to 2 days ahead and keep covered in the fridge.
- If serving with Melba toast, this can be made a week or more in advance and stored in an airtight container. It pretty much lasts forever, if the container is completely airtight, so it's worth making more than you need, as it's a useful standby.

## Hints & Tips

- The mousse doesn't have to be turned out. Make it in a pretty glass or china bowl and pass around for people to help themselves. This is good for transporting to picnics, too.
- Gelatine loses its setting qualities if boiled, so always add it off the heat and when the stock has had time to cool a little.

# TUNA & AVOCADO CEVICHE

SERVES 4

2 spring onions, trimmed, halved and finely sliced lengthways
225–255g (8–9oz) very fresh tuna (1 or 2 steaks)
1 scant tbsp sushi ginger, thinly sliced
½ red chilli, seeded and finely sliced
½ green chilli, seeded and finely sliced
1 medium avocado or ½ a large one
a few leaves of coriander or flat-leaf parsley
black and/or white sesame seeds, toasted, for sprinkling

FOR THE DRESSING
scant ½ tbsp granulated sugar
2 tbsp fish sauce
freshly squeezed juice of 1 lime (approximately 2 tbsp)
1 small clove of garlic, crushed

**A lovely light, fresh starter and just the job before a substantial main course. It's very good for lunch, too, especially when served with griddled bread (see page 22).**

**1.** Put the strips of spring onion into a small bowl. Cover with water and then clingfilm, and put in the fridge for a minimum of 30 minutes or up to 24 hours.

**2.** Mix all the dressing ingredients together and set aside, giving it the occasional stir to help dissolve the sugar.

**3.** Slice the tuna thinly across the grain and arrange in the middle of four individual plates (approximately 5 slices per plate).

**4.** Scatter the ginger and chillies over the tuna. Cut the avocado, within its skin into small dice using a round-bladed knife and divide it between the four plates, piling it up in the middle of the tuna. Drain the spring onion, dry on kitchen paper and pile on top of the avocado. Arrange 4–5 leaves of coriander or parsley around the edges of each plate.

**5.** Just before serving, spoon over the dressing and scatter with the sesame seeds.

**Get Ahead**

- Prepare the spring onions, ginger, chillies and dressing up to 24 hours in advance.
- Slice the tuna up to 24 hours ahead, re-form and keep in the fridge, tightly wrapped in clingfilm.
- At any time on the day, arrange the tuna on the plates, cover with clingfilm, stack up and store in the fridge until required.
- Prepare to the end of step 4 up to 2 hours ahead, cover and keep somewhere cool.

**Hints & Tips**

It is best to use an avocado that is only just ripe, as it won't go brown nearly as quickly as a very ripe one will. In the case of the latter, don't cut until just before serving.

# DEVILLED CRAB

SERVES 6

450g (1lb) very fresh white crab meat (or white and brown mixed)
⅛–¼ tsp cayenne pepper
1 tsp Worcestershire sauce
1 tsp freshly squeezed lemon juice
1 tsp Dijon mustard
2 tsp anchovy essence
2 tbsp freshly chopped parsley
150ml (5fl oz) double cream or crème fraîche
2 tbsp grated Parmesan cheese
2 tbsp breadcrumbs, dried or fresh
salt and freshly ground black pepper

**Get Ahead**

Make to the end of step 3 up to 2 days in advance, cover and refrigerate, or freeze. Thaw for a few hours before cooking.

**Crab is one of my top five favourite things to eat. We get fabulous crab here in north Northumberland, straight from the North Sea. This is such a tasty, piquant way to cook it, albeit old-fashioned, but there's nothing wrong with that in my book. It's just as good for lunch, served with crusty bread and a salad.**

**1.** Preheat the oven to 200°C.

**2.** Mix all the ingredients, except for the cheese and breadcrumbs, together well. Check the seasoning – it should be quite spicy and well seasoned.

**3.** Divide the mixture between 6 ramekins or small ovenproof dishes. Sprinkle with the cheese and breadcrumbs.

**4.** Bake in the preheated oven for 7–10 minutes or until golden brown.

# POTTED PRAWNS



SERVES 6

**450g (1lb) cooked peeled prawns, thawed weight (frozen weight approximately 525g/18oz)**
**150g (6oz) butter**
**¼ tsp curry powder**
**¼ tsp ground mace**
**¼ tsp grated nutmeg**
**¼ tsp salt**
**freshly ground black pepper**

SERVING SUGGESTIONS
**Lemon or lime wedges, bay leaves, fresh dill, cooked large prawns, Melba toast (see below right) or toast**

**You can't beat a classic!**

**1.** Drain the prawns and spread out on kitchen paper to absorb any excess liquid.

**2.** Clarify the butter by melting it gently in a small saucepan. Skim the white scum off the top and discard. Carefully pour the butter into a measuring jug, leaving behind and discarding the milky sediment at the bottom.

**3.** In a bowl, mix roughly half the clarified butter with all the remaining ingredients. Add the prawns and mix together, making sure they are evenly coated.

**4.** Pack fairly tightly into six pretty ramekins, small coffee cups, dariole moulds or one large bowl. Press down to level the tops and spoon over the remainder of the clarified butter. Chill in the fridge until set.

**5.** Serve lukewarm, turned out or in their pots.

## Get Ahead

- The prawns will last for 3 days, covered, in the fridge.
- **Melba toast:** Toast 6–9 slices of bread and cut the crusts off. Carefully slice each one in half horizontally through the middle with a serrated bread knife, using a gentle sawing motion. Open out, put the slices toasted-side down on a baking sheet and bake at 200°C for 3–5 minutes or until golden brown and curled up around the edges. Allow 2–3 pieces per person. It will keep almost indefinitely in an airtight container.

## Hints & Tips

- Small bay leaves can be set in the bottom of each mould before filling with the prawns.
- This looks very good made in a round-bottomed mixing bowl, turned out and served as a starter, or as a centrepiece for a fishy, buffet-style platter, surrounded by wavy slices of smoked salmon, gravadlax, smoked eel and/or shellfish.

# PARMA HAM, GOAT'S CHEESE & PESTO PARCELS WITH CARAMELIZED PECANS

SERVES 4 AS A STARTER OR 2 FOR LUNCH

**a little olive oil**
**a handful of pecan nuts**
**runny honey**
**4 little 'branches' of small cherry tomatoes on the vine – about 3 per branch (optional)**
**8 thin slices of Parma ham, straight from the fridge**
**100g (3½oz) whole goat's cheese, with skin**
**4 tsp pesto sauce**
**rocket and/or watercress leaves, lightly dressed**
**balsamic syrup and chives (optional, see Hints & Tips, below right)**
**salt**

### Get Ahead

- Make to the end of step 5 up to a day ahead, cover and keep in the fridge. The parcels can be left in the fridge on the silicone paper or non-stick baking sheet, ready to go straight into the oven.
- The pecans can be caramelized several days in advance and stored in an airtight container, where they will keep fresh for a few weeks.

**Despite being a hot starter, these tasty little 'money bags' can be made the day before and are quick and easy to cook and assemble when you're ready to eat.**

**1.** Preheat the oven to 220°C. Oil or line a baking sheet with silicone/baking paper.

**2.** Mix the pecans in a bowl with just enough honey to coat them all, then cook the nuts in a frying pan, stirring until golden and caramelized. Once they begin to caramelize, they burn very quickly, so beware! Tip out and spread out immediately on the prepared baking sheet and leave to cool.

**3.** If using, put the tomatoes onto a small baking sheet, scatter with olive oil and salt, and cook in the preheated oven for about 5 minutes until just cooked and wilting, but still holding their shape.

**4.** Oil a baking sheet, or line with silicone paper. Place two pieces of Parma ham on the worktop, overlapping at right angles, to form a cross. Repeat with the rest.

**5.** Cut the goat's cheese into four equal discs (1cm/½in thick), place a disc in the middle of each cross, then top with a teaspoon of pesto sauce. Bring the four edges of Parma ham up over the cheese, gathering it at the top and pinching it together to form a money-bag shape. Place on the prepared baking sheet.

**6.** Drizzle with a little olive oil and bake for 5 minutes or until beginning to turn brown and crispy. Some of the cheese may ooze out but that is part of the charm!

**7.** Serve (complete with oozy bits) on individual plates with the lightly dressed leaves to one side, a bunch of tomatoes, if using, and a few caramelized pecan nuts scattered over. A trickle of balsamic syrup around the edge of the plate and over the salad adds to both the taste and appearance, as do a few chopped chives.

### Hints & Tips

- Parma ham is impossible to work with unless used straight from the fridge. It is worth having a couple of extra slices in case you need it for running repairs around the edges of the money bags.
- You can buy the balsamic syrup, but the homemade variety tastes far superior and lasts almost indefinitely. Boil some balsamic vinegar rapidly in a small saucepan until reduced by about half. It should have become slightly syrupy, but bear in mind that it will thicken up considerably when cold and will *not* be thick and syrupy in the pan. I store it in a chef's squeezy bottle as the nozzle provides the perfect squirty distributor. Alternatively, a thumb positioned over the top of an old tonic bottle will do just as well.

# GAZPACHO WITH TAPENADE BREADSTICKS

SERVES 10–12

**2 red peppers, quartered and seeded**
**1 large cucumber**
**1 large or 2 small onions**
**900g (2lb) very ripe tomatoes**
**2 large cloves of garlic, peeled**
**1 slice of white bread, soaked in water and squeezed out**
**125ml (4fl oz) olive oil**
**1 tbsp sherry or red wine vinegar**
**400g (14oz) tin chopped tomatoes or passata**
**1 tbsp tomato purée**
**1 tsp sugar**
**2 tsp salt**
**freshly ground black pepper**

GARNISH SUGGESTIONS

**Very finely diced red pepper, cucumber and black olives, finely sliced spring onions (or thin strips curled in cold water), ground black pepper and a few drops of olive oil, tiny croutons, chives, mint or basil leaves**

### Hints & Tips

- The vegetable quantities are flexible, so just use the recipe as a guide.
- This will taste different every time you make it. The quality of the vegetables determines the final result. As with all food to be eaten cold, the flavour will be dulled when chilled, so bear this in mind when seasoning at the outset and check again before eating.

**Gazpacho is perfect as a starter or for a picnic on a hot summer's day, or served in shot glasses as a 'canapé', possibly with a nip of vodka. Fresh, healthy and easy, it requires no cooking, is an inexpensive way to feed a crowd and is a summer glut-guzzler, too.**

**1.** Very finely dice a small amount of red pepper and cucumber if using as a garnish, and set aside. Roughly cut the remaining vegetables and garlic into chunks, and combine in a large mixing bowl.

**2.** The soup will need to be blitzed in two batches, so crumble half the bread into a liquidizer with half of the rest of the ingredients (the garlic, vegetables, olive oil, vinegar, tinned tomatoes or passata, tomato purée and seasoning), and blitz to a purée. Sieve into a large bowl and then repeat with the remaining ingredients. Check the seasoning and thin with a little cold water if it's too thick.

**3.** Chill for at least 6 hours (overnight is best) or until required. Gazpacho must be served very cold.

**4.** Ladle into individual bowls, cups or shot glasses and float your chosen garnishes on top (see left).

### Get Ahead

Make to the end of step 3 up to 2 days ahead. It will last for several days in the fridge.

## TAPENADE BREADSTICKS

MAKES 15–18 LONG STICKS

**1 ciabatta loaf**
**5–6 tbsp olive oil**
**3 tbsp tapenade**
**sea salt flakes**
**hot smoked paprika**

**1.** Preheat the oven to 220°C.

**2.** Slice a loaf of ciabatta into thirds horizontally. Mix the olive oil with the tapenade and brush over the top of the slices. Slice each piece into 5 or 6 long sticks, depending on loaf size, and space out on a baking sheet. Sprinkle with sea salt flakes and a little smoked paprika.

**3.** Bake in the preheated oven for 5–8 minutes or until golden brown and crisp.

**4.** Store in an airtight container for a week or so. Heat through before using to freshen and crisp up. Serve in a pretty vase or glasses, or criss-crossed in a grid à la Jenga.

Ⓥ

# CHILLED PEA, CUMIN & CORIANDER SOUP

SERVES 8–10

1–2 tbsp olive oil
1 large onion, roughly chopped
½ tsp ground cumin
1 litre (1¾ pint) vegetable or chicken stock (or use 2 stock cubes)
900g (2lb) frozen peas
55g (2oz) fresh coriander
100ml (3½fl oz) single or double cream (optional)
salt and freshly ground black pepper

SERVING SUGGESTIONS

A dollop of crème fraîche or swirl of cream, a few peas, a sprig of coriander or pea shoots, crispy fried pancetta, Parma ham or thinly sliced chorizo, complete with its oil, small fried croutons, shredded ham hock, tapenade breadsticks (see page 34)

**A lovely vibrant green colour, fresh with a hint of spice, this soup is better than the sum of its parts, and one of my favourites. Try it and see…**

**1.** Heat the olive oil in a saucepan and cook the onion until beginning to soften but not brown. Add the cumin, fry for another minute and then add the stock (or stock cubes and water). Bring to the boil and simmer for 15 minutes or until the onion is soft.

**2.** Keeping a few aside for a garnish, add the peas and coriander leaves and stalks. Season with salt and pepper and bring just back to the boil.

**3.** Liquidize immediately and sieve into a bowl. It may need thinning with a little cold water to the desired consistency, although bear in mind that the cream, if using, will also thin it a little. Cool, cover and refrigerate until chilled (overnight is best).

**4.** Stir in the cream (if using) and serve garnished with any of the serving suggestions (see left).

### Get Ahead

Make 2–3 days in advance. A thin layer on top of the soup may turn a murky colour, but it will still be a vibrant green underneath (just skim it off or stir it in). This soup freezes beautifully; however, if eating chilled, it will need to be whisked back to a smooth consistency once thawed.

### Hints & Tips

This soup tastes delicious hot, too. Heat to just under boiling point and serve straightaway. The more it's reheated, the more it will lose its colour.

# WILD GARLIC SOUP



(V)

SERVES 8

2 tbsp olive oil
1 large onion, chopped
1 large potato, peeled and roughly chopped
1.2 litres (2 pints) vegetable or chicken stock (or use 3 stock cubes)
170g (6oz) wild garlic leaves
cream (optional)
wild garlic flowers (optional)
salt and freshly ground black pepper

**You can't beat this soup in the wild garlic season, from the end of March to the end of June. Bright green and nutritious, it's also free, if you're lucky enough to find it growing in woodland and damp shady spots. It's common to most woodland and you will most likely smell it before you see it.**

**1.** Heat the oil in a large saucepan, add the onion and potato, and cook until beginning to soften but not colour.

**2.** Add the stock (or stock cubes and water), bring to the boil and simmer for 20 minutes or until the potato is cooked. Check the seasoning.

**3.** Set aside a few wild garlic leaves to garnish and add the rest to the soup. Stir until just wilted. Purée the soup using a liquidizer or hand blender, adding some cream to taste, if using. You might like to save some cream to swirl in just before serving.

**4.** Stack the reserved leaves on top of each other and roll into a cigarette shape. Shred into very thin ribbons using a large chopping knife.

**5.** Serve the soup in bowls, topped with a swirl of cream, the shredded leaves and the flowers, if using.

### Get Ahead

Make to the end of step 3 up to 2 days in advance and refrigerate or freeze.

### Hints & Tips

- You may need to thin the soup by adding a little stock or water. It should be very well seasoned.
- A tablespoon of grated Parmesan cheese stirred in at the last minute is delicious and takes the soup to another level.

# CHICORY, ROQUEFORT & WALNUT SALAD

SERVES 4 AS A STARTER
OR 2 AS A MAIN COURSE

2 large heads of chicory (white, red or both)
85g (3oz) Roquefort cheese
a handful of walnut halves or pieces
a handful of watercress
sea salt and freshly ground black pepper
walnut or olive oil

**I make this starter more than any other when entertaining. Crisp and refreshing, with the slight bitterness of the chicory offset by the blue cheese and walnuts, it also happens to be one of my favourite things to eat.**

**1.** Discard any soft or damaged outer leaves from the chicory. Separate some of the outer leaves and arrange 4–6 large whole leaves on each of four big plates for a starter, or 8–12 leaves on two plates for a main course. Thinly slice the remaining chicory hearts vertically and scatter these slices over the leaves.

**2.** Crumble the blue cheese over the top, followed by the walnuts, and nestle a few sprigs of watercress in between the chicory.

**3.** Just before serving, sprinkle with sea salt, a grinding of black pepper and a swirl or two of walnut or olive oil.

### Get Ahead

Prepare to the end of step 2 up to 2 hours in advance.

### Hints & Tips

- Any creamy or crumbly blue cheese can be substituted. Choose a vegetarian alternative, such as Stilton or Dolcelatte, if required.
- Accompanied by roasted chicken legs, this is a favourite supper. Rub the chicken with olive oil and salt, and cook for 35 minutes in a hot oven until golden, crispy and cooked through. Simple yet perfect!

# JERUSALEM ARTICHOKE, BACON & MUSHROOM COCOTTES

SERVES 6

**450g (1lb) Jerusalem artichokes**
**a squeeze of fresh lemon juice**
**4 rashers of smoked streaky bacon, snipped into thin strips**
**110g (4oz) chestnut mushrooms, sliced**
**1 clove of garlic, crushed**
**a few fresh sage leaves**
**olive oil**
**150ml (5fl oz) double cream**
**1 tsp Dijon mustard**
**3 tbsp grated Parmesan cheese**
**2 tbsp dried breadcrumbs**
**Jerusalem artichoke crisps, to garnish (optional, see Hints & Tips, below right)**
**salt and freshly ground black pepper**

**Deeply flavourful, earthy and warming, and just the job for an autumnal day.**

**1.** Preheat the oven to 220°C.

**2.** Scrub the artichokes well. Add to a pan of water with a squeeze of lemon juice to prevent them from discolouring, bring to the boil and simmer for 10 minutes, or until only just tender. The time will depend on their size, but they should be slightly underdone and not bursting out of their skins. Drain and run under cold water until cool enough to handle.

**3.** If the skins are thin, pale-coloured and unblemished, the artichokes won't need peeling. If not, carefully pull away the skins with a knife. It doesn't matter if some flesh crumbles a little. Slice into rounds, roughly the thickness of a £1 coin, and halve any large discs. Transfer to a mixing bowl.

**4.** Dry-fry the strips of bacon until golden brown and crisp. Add to the artichokes. Fry the mushrooms, garlic and sage in the residual fat in the bacon pan (add a smidgen of olive oil, if necessary), season well and fry fast until all the moisture has evaporated and they begin to brown. Add to the artichokes and gently amalgamate everything. Divide between six ovenproof dishes or ramekins.

**5.** Mix the cream, Dijon mustard and some seasoning together, and spoon into the dishes. Scatter with the grated Parmesan cheese and dried breadcrumbs.

**6.** Bake in the oven for 10–15 minutes or until golden brown and bubbling. Garnish with Jerusalem artichoke crisps, if using (see Hints & Tips, below right).

### Get Ahead

The cocottes can be made to the end of step 5 up to 24 hours in advance, covered and refrigerated until required. Remember to bring them back to room temperature for at least an hour before cooking.

### Hints & Tips

**Jerusalem artichoke crisps:** Peel (only if the skin is dark and tough) 2–4 raw Jerusalem artichokes and slice very thinly. Fry immediately in a little olive oil for a few minutes until golden and quite crisp; they will crisp up more as they cool. Drain well on scrunched-up kitchen paper and sprinkle with salt. Make up to 3 days ahead.

# ·BRUNCHING· & LUNCHING

# PARMESAN & BLACK OLIVE SODA BREAD

SERVES 6–8

**225g (8oz) plain flour**
**225g (8oz) wholemeal flour**
**1 tsp bicarbonate of soda**
**2 tsp cream of tartar**
**1 tsp salt**
**55g (2oz) Parmesan cheese, grated, plus a little extra for the top (see tip, page 10)**
**12 stoned black olives, roughly chopped**
**1 tbsp olive oil**
**225g (8oz) natural yoghurt**
**190ml (6fl oz) milk**

**A savoury twist on the classic Irish soda bread, which is one of the simplest breads to make as it contains no yeast and doesn't require proving. Very good with most things, particularly soup and cold meats, it also makes tasty canapé bases.**

1. Preheat the oven to 190°C.

2. In a large bowl sift together the flours, bicarbonate of soda, cream of tartar and salt. Add the Parmesan and olives.

3. Mix together the olive oil and yoghurt and stir into the dry ingredients with a wooden spoon. Add enough milk to make a soft dough. You may not need it all.

4. Knead together gently with your hands, just to bring the dough together, no more, as it should not be overworked. Transfer to a baking sheet and shape into a round. Press the handle of a wooden spoon down into the dough to make a shallow cross, or wedge shapes, over the top.

5. Scatter with a little grated Parmesan and bake in the preheated oven for 45 minutes. Dust with a little wholemeal flour and cool on a wire rack.

### Get Ahead

- Weigh and prepare all ingredients up to 48 hours in advance, but don't mix until you are ready to bake.
- Like all bread, this is best eaten on the day it's made. If not eating straightaway, keep well wrapped for several days or freeze. After thawing, briefly warm through in the oven.

### Hints & Tips

- The bread can also be made in a greased 900g (2lb) loaf tin. Leave to cool in the tin for a few minutes before turning out onto a wire rack.
- This makes an excellent savoury base for canapés. Slice the bread, cut out small rounds with a pastry cutter, put on a baking sheet, scatter with a little sea salt and olive oil, and bake until golden and crisp. If not using straightaway, freeze until required and warm through to freshen up before using. Once topped, these stay crisp for far longer than regular, thinner croûtes. Very handy!

# PEA, MINT & PECORINO BRUSCHETTA



MAKES 6–8 (DEPENDING ON THE SIZE OF THE BREAD)

**200g (7oz) fresh or frozen peas**
**2 sprigs of mint, leaves only**
**1–2 tsp crème fraîche**
**6–8 slices of sourdough, ciabatta or artisan-style bread, sliced diagonally**
**1 clove of garlic, peeled**
**olive oil**
**3 spring onions, trimmed and sliced diagonally into thin rings**
**a little Pecorino cheese, for shaving**
**nigella seeds, pea shoots and/or small, pretty salad leaves or salad cress, for serving**
**sea salt and freshly ground black pepper**

**These are just perfect for a warm day, especially when arranged on a pretty platter. A few slices of Parma ham or smoked salmon draped in between the bruschettas make a more substantial lunch or supper.**

1. Put the peas and some salt into a pan, barely cover with boiling water and as soon as it starts to come to the boil, drain and cool.

2. Purée the cooled peas with the mint leaves and some seasoning in a small processor or with a hand blender, leaving a bit of texture to the purée. Add the crème fraîche a teaspoon at a time, bearing in mind the purée will be spooned onto the bread – you might not need it all. Taste and adjust the seasoning accordingly – it should be well seasoned.

3. Toast or griddle the bread on both sides, rub with the garlic and put onto a board, a large serving platter or individual plates. Drizzle over a little olive oil and top with the pea purée. Scatter over the spring onions and some Pecorino shavings. Decorate with a sprinkling of nigella seeds, a few pea shoots and/or salad leaves or cress, plus a final swirl of olive oil, and a sprinkling of sea salt flakes.

### Get Ahead

- Steps 1 and 2 can be made up to 2 days ahead.
- If using sourdough, the bruschettas can be assembled up to 1½–2 hours ahead. After that they will become slightly less crisp in the middle. However, the length of time they remain crisp rather depends on the bread.

### Hints & Tips

- Serve warm or at room temperature. Cut large slices of bread in half before adding the topping.
- Substitute broad beans for the peas and Parmesan for the Pecorino.

# CHORIZO HASH

SERVES 4

**olive oil**
**1 large onion, sliced**
**6 fresh chorizo sausages**
**2 cloves of garlic, crushed**
**a good pinch of dried oregano**
**½ tsp hot smoked paprika**
**675g (1½lb) waxy new potatoes, cooked and cut into rough chunks**
**100g (3½oz) baby spinach**
**4 eggs**
**a few sprigs of parsley, chopped**
**nigella seeds, Tabasco or sriracha sauce (optional)**
**salt and freshly ground black pepper**

**A little bit spicy, very comforting, all in one pan and an excellent way of using up leftover potatoes. Good for brunch, lunch or supper and perfect for the morning after the night before! All quantities are approximate, so use more or less according to who you're feeding and what you have to hand.**

1. Heat a little olive oil in a sauté or deep frying pan and cook the onion until soft and just beginning to brown. Slice each sausage diagonally into approximately six slices and add to the onions. Fry over a high heat until beginning to brown and the red juices are running from the chorizo.

2. Add the garlic, oregano, smoked paprika and potatoes, and season with salt and black pepper. Gently mix together and, when sizzling vigorously, cover with a lid and cook over a lower heat for 10 minutes. The mixture should only just be sizzling very gently.

3. Add the spinach and nestle in until just wilted.

4. Fry the eggs in a little olive oil in a separate frying pan, or poach them, and serve on top of the hash with a good scattering of parsley. Add nigella seeds and a few drops of Tabasco or sriracha sauce, if you wish.

### Get Ahead

Cook to the end of step 2 up to a day in advance. If preparing on the day, just leave in the pan and continue when required.

### Hints & Tips

- Some people might like two eggs!
- Try using soft semi-dried salami-style chorizo in place of fresh chorizo.
- Use regular paprika and a pinch of chilli powder if you don't have hot smoked paprika.

# ASPARAGUS, PEA, MINT & GOAT'S CHEESE FRITTATA

SERVES 4–6

**a splash of olive oil**
**1 onion, sliced**
**1 clove of garlic, crushed**
**170g (6oz) peas, cooked**
**a generous sprig of mint, leaves roughly snipped or chopped**
**8 eggs, lightly beaten with a fork**
**a knob of butter**
**100g (3½oz) whole goat's cheese with skin**
**12 asparagus tips, cooked until just tender**
**1 tbsp grated Parmesan cheese**
**salt and freshly ground black pepper**

**A lovely frittata for spring or early summer, celebrating the new season's vibrant green asparagus and peas, with the fresh kick of mint. Serve with a green salad and a tomato and onion salad.**

1. Preheat the oven to 200°C.

2. Heat the oil in a deepish, preferably ovenproof, frying pan (ideally, 20 x 4.5cm/ 8 x 1¾in) and cook the onion until soft and beginning to colour a little. Add the garlic and cook for a further minute.

3. Add the peas, mint and some seasoning to the beaten eggs, followed by the cooked onion. Mix well together.

4. Wipe out the frying pan, melt the butter and add the egg mixture. Cook over a medium heat until the bottom is golden and the egg has set around the edges and about halfway through its depth. This will take 5–10 minutes, depending on the depth of the pan.

5. Slice the cheese into four discs, then tear each one in half and arrange over the top of the unset egg mixture. Arrange the asparagus tips over the top in a cartwheel pattern, sprinkle with Parmesan and cook in the preheated oven for 10–15 minutes, or until barely set in the middle. Leave to stand for 5–10 minutes. Serve from the pan, or loosen with a palette knife and slide onto a serving plate.

### Get Ahead

Prepare to the end of step 3 at any time on the day. The peas and asparagus can be cooked up to 2 days ahead.

### Hints & Tips

- If using a larger, shallower frying pan, bear in mind that a shorter cooking time will be needed.
- For a picnic, or for a rustic appearance, serve the frittata on a sheet of greaseproof or baking paper.
- If using a non-ovenproof frying pan, finish off under the grill, preheated to its highest setting.
- This is delicious cut into small bite-sized pieces and served cold as canapés with drinks.

Ⓥ

# SCRAMBLED EGGS WITH A TWIST

SERVES 2

butter (for frying and for buttering the toast)
3 spring onions or 1 shallot, thinly sliced
½ a red or green chilli, seeded and finely chopped, or a pinch of dried chilli flakes
1 clove of garlic, crushed
2 good slices of bread (ideally, sourdough)
4–6 eggs
salt and freshly ground black pepper

ADDITIONAL OPTIONAL FILLINGS

1 tomato, quartered, seeded and diced
freshly chopped coriander, parsley or chives
a handful of wild garlic or spinach leaves, cut into thin ribbons
a little grated Parmesan cheese

**Loosely based on spicy Sri Lankan omelettes and Indian egg dishes, these are scrambled eggs with knobs on! Moreish, with a little bit of heat and oodles of flavour, they are just the job for breakfast, brunch or a light supper – a great Sunday night staple.**

1. Melt a little butter in a saucepan and cook the onion and chilli until softened. Add the garlic and cook briefly until fragrant.

2. Meanwhile, toast and butter the bread. Keep warm.

3. Off the heat, break the eggs into the saucepan and break up/scramble with a wooden spoon. Cook over a gentle heat, stirring continuously. Keep moving the pan on and off the heat, still stirring, to prevent the eggs from overcooking. They should be creamy and barely set.

4. Just before the eggs are cooked to your liking, season and stir in any, or all of, the additional ingredients (see left), except for the Parmesan. Cook to your preferred consistency, and then spoon onto the toast. Scatter with Parmesan, if using, and serve immediately.

**Get Ahead**

Prepare to the end of step 1 up to 24 hours ahead.

**Hints & Tips**

- Increase the amount of chilli if you like it hot.
- As always when scrambling eggs, to ensure big curds and a lovely texture, don't add any salt until the very last minute.

# OMELETTE ARNOLD BENNETT – MY WAY!

SERVES 4

340g (12oz) undyed smoked haddock
1 bay leaf
200ml (7fl oz) milk
55g (2oz) butter
30g (1oz) plain flour
2 tbsp cream, plus a little extra
200g (7oz) baby spinach, cooked and squeezed of excess liquid
6 eggs
a little grated Parmesan cheese
salt and freshly ground black pepper

**This is one of the tastiest imaginable egg dishes – what could be more delicious than eggs, smoked haddock, spinach and cheese? In fact, traditional Omelette Arnold Bennett doesn't have spinach in it, but as I love eggs and spinach together, plus the fact that it is good for you and gives some nice colour, I like to add it to my version. Traditionally, this is a soufflé omelette, made lighter with the addition of whisked egg whites. However, I have deconstructed and simplified it somewhat, making it quicker to produce than the original.**

1. Put the haddock into a small saucepan with the bay leaf and milk. Bring slowly to the boil and then take off the heat immediately. When cool enough to handle, strain into a jug and flake the fish, removing any skin and bones, but keeping it chunky. Discard the bay leaf.

2. For the sauce, melt half the butter in a saucepan, mix in the flour, cook for a minute, season, then gradually stir in the strained milk and bring to the boil. The sauce will be very thick. Remove from the heat. Stir in the cream and cooked spinach, then very gently add the haddock, trying not to break it up too much.

3. Heat the grill to its highest setting.

4. Lightly beat the eggs with a fork. Melt the remaining butter in a 23–25cm (9–10in) frying pan, add the eggs and cook as you would normally for an omelette by pulling the mixture into the middle from the edge. When the eggs have nearly but not quite all set, spread the haddock sauce evenly over the top. Scatter with some Parmesan and a swirl of cream and cook under the grill for a few minutes until golden brown and bubbling.

### Get Ahead

Make to the end of step 2 up to 2 days in advance, cool, cover and chill until required.

### Hints & Tips

I like to serve this with a tomato salad and perhaps a green salad and some good bread, too.

# COURGETTE, PARMESAN & MINT FRITTERS

MAKES APPROXIMATELY 16 THIN FRITTERS

**2 medium courgettes**
**2 tbsp self-raising flour**
**2 tbsp grated Parmesan cheese**
**2 eggs, lightly beaten**
**2 sprigs of mint, leaves chopped**
**2 spring onions, trimmed and chopped**
**salt and freshly ground black pepper**
**olive oil**
**sea salt**
**See below right for topping suggestions**

### Get Ahead

- Step 1 can be completed at any time on the day.
- The fritters can be cooked in advance and eaten cold or reheated.

**A delicious way of eating courgettes, and of using up a glut! Serve as an accompaniment to almost anything – they're particularly good with lamb, fish and chicken or just with a salad for lunch. We sometimes substitute them for potatoes. They're also very good as a starter, with a topping or a salsa (see ideas below). Make them smaller and they morph into lovely summery canapés.**

1. Grate the courgettes as coarsely as you like (it is easiest to do this in a food processor). Put into a sieve, sprinkle with a little salt and leave to drain for 30 minutes. Squeeze out the excess liquid and put the courgettes in a mixing bowl with the rest of the ingredients, except the olive oil and sea salt. Mix together well.

2. Heat a little oil in a frying pan and dollop in dessertspoons of the mixture, spreading and flattening with the back of the spoon. Cook in batches, and do not overcrowd the pan or they will stew rather than fry. After a minute or two, when the underside is golden, flip over and cook for another minute or so.

3. Remove, drain on kitchen paper and sprinkle with a little sea salt. Keep the batches warm while cooking the rest. Serve as is, or with any of the suggested toppings below.

### Topping Suggestions

- Minty yoghurt
- Garlicky mayonnaise
- Gravadlax or Beetroot & Fennel Cured Salmon with Horseradish Sauce or Cucumber & Dill Sauce and Cucumber Ribbons with Fennel Shavings (see page 65)
- Smoked salmon or hot smoked salmon with crème fraîche, chives or chopped onion and optional Avruga 'caviar'
- Feta cheese and black olives or tapenade
- Salsas of any description, such as tomato, red pepper, onion, chilli, herbs and vinegar
- Guacamole
- Soft goat's cheese with chives, sumac or pink peppercorns
- White crab meat with finely chopped red chilli and possibly a little mayonnaise
- Greek yoghurt or labneh (see page 24) with dukkah or ras el hanout for a Moroccan flavour

pie

# THE FULL-ENGLISH PICNIC PIE

MAKES 24 SMALLISH SQUARES FOR A PICNIC, OR 8–12 LARGER ONES FOR LUNCH OR BRUNCH

**500g (1lb 2oz) block of shortcrust pastry**
**16 rashers of streaky bacon, snipped into 2.5cm (1in) chunks**
**450g (1lb) chestnut mushrooms, cut into thickish slices**
**olive oil**
**200g (7oz) black pudding, thinly sliced**
**10 eggs, plus 1 for egg wash**
**nigella seeds**
**sea salt flakes**
**salt and freshly ground black pepper**

### Get Ahead

Prepare to the end of step 6, cover and refrigerate up to 24 hours in advance. Bring back to room temperature an hour or so before cooking. Continue with step 7. The filling ingredients can be cooked several days in advance.

### Hints & Tips

- Eat warm or at room temperature, but not piping hot.
- Serve with puréed piccalilli, sriracha sauce, mayo, mustard, ketchup or little bunches of roasted tomatoes on the vine (see Hints & Tips, page 114).
- Substitute cooked sausages cut into chunks for the black pudding, or spinach for the bacon and black pudding for a vegetarian pie.

**Be it for brunch, lunch or a picnic, 'The Full English' in a pie is such a useful recipe to have up your sleeve. Better still, you can assemble it entirely the day before and cook it when you wake up!**

1. Preheat the oven to 180°C. Line a baking tin or ovenproof dish (approximately 30 x 20 x 5cm/12 x 8 x 2¼in) with baking paper, mitring the corners. (Using foil-lined baking paper makes this job easier.)

2. Cut the pastry roughly in half, with one piece very slightly larger, and roll the latter out large enough to line the tin (approximately 40 x 30cm/16 x 12in). You may need to cut and patchwork the pastry for some areas, and some might overlap the edges. Chill for 30 minutes.

3. Fry the bacon in a dry pan until it begins to brown and crisp. Drain on kitchen paper. Add the mushrooms to the residual bacon fat (add a little extra oil if necessary), season well and cook quickly until all the liquid has evaporated and they begin to brown. Remove and set aside to cool. Add a smidge of oil to the unwashed pan and cook the black pudding for 1–2 minutes on both sides. Transfer to a plate to cool.

4. Spread the mushrooms over the bottom of the chilled pastry, followed by the bacon and then the black pudding, breaking it up for even coverage. Break the eggs over the top, spacing them as evenly as possible. Don't worry if the odd yolk breaks. Season with a grinding of pepper.

5. Lightly beat the remaining egg with a little salt. Roll out the rest of the pastry, large enough to fit as a lid. Brush the edges of the overhanging base pastry with the egg wash and carefully sit the lid over the top. Trim off the excess pastry and crimp the edges together.

6. If you wish, re-roll the pastry trimmings and cut out for decoration, such as the word 'pie', leaves, hearts and so on. Brush the lid with egg wash and sprinkle with nigella seeds. Brush both sides of any pastry decoration with a little egg wash and glue it to the top.

7. Sprinkle with a few flakes of sea salt and bake in the preheated oven for 40 minutes or until crispy and golden brown.

# SIZZLING CRISPY LAMB SALAD

SERVES 4–6 FOR LUNCH
OR 6–8 AS A STARTER

**1 breast of lamb, on the bone**
**18–24 cherry or baby plum tomatoes (approximately 3 per person)**
**olive oil**
**a pinch of dried oregano or the leaves of two sprigs, chopped**
**4 good handfuls of watercress**
**4 small handfuls of mixed salad leaves or a round/butterhead lettuce**
**½ red onion, very thinly sliced**
**2 tbsp small capers**
**4 sprigs of mint, leaves finely sliced**
**salad cress**
**sea salt and freshly ground black pepper**

FOR THE DRESSING
**½ tsp salt**
**1 tbsp water**
**½ tbsp sherry vinegar**
**1 tbsp raspberry vinegar**
**5 tbsp olive oil**

### Get Ahead

Prepare to the end of step 2 up to a week in advance and keep wrapped in clingfilm in the fridge, or freeze. Steps 3 and 4 can be prepared up to 3 days ahead. The rashers can be sliced (step 5) at any time on the day of eating.

**Mouthwatering crispy lamb rashers with a tangy, crunchy salad. Better still, breast of lamb is an incredibly cheap cut of meat. This is very good as a starter or, if bulked up a little, as a main-course salad. The recipe needs starting the day before.**

1. Preheat the oven to 160°C.

2. Season the lamb and cook in a shallow, foil-lined roasting tin for 2½ hours. While still warm, pull out the bones by twisting them and remove the arc-shaped piece of white cartilage behind them. Sandwich the meat between two sheets of baking or greaseproof paper, or clingfilm, and press between two baking trays or boards, with weights (such as tins) on top. Refrigerate when cold.

3. Preheat the oven to 220°C. Put the tomatoes onto a baking sheet lined with foil, scatter with a little olive oil, oregano, sea salt and black pepper, and cook for 10–12 minutes or until just beginning to wilt but still holding together. The skins will have burst and the tomatoes may be a little charred, which is all the better for that rustic taste and charm. Set aside. Leave the oven on.

4. Whisk the dressing ingredients together.

5. Peel off any visible membrane and excess fat from the lamb and slice into thin rashers (roughly 5mm/¼in thick). Put onto a foil-lined baking sheet, sprinkle with salt and cook in the hot oven for 5–10 minutes or until turning golden and crispy. Drain on scrunched-up kitchen paper.

6. Put the watercress and salad leaves in the middle of individual plates or one large platter, and arrange the lamb over the top. You may like to cut it into shorter rashers. Dot the tomatoes around and scatter over the red onion and some capers. Spoon over a little dressing and finally scatter over the mint and some snipped salad cress.

# CHICORY, BLUE CHEESE, BACON & WALNUT GRATIN

SERVES 4

**4 heads of chicory**
**4 rashers of smoked streaky bacon, cut into thin strips**
**55g (2oz) butter**
**40g (1½oz) creamy blue cheese, crumbled**
**a handful of walnuts, roughly chopped**
**walnut oil (optional)**
**a few parsley leaves, roughly chopped**
**salt and freshly ground black pepper**

**Meltingly soft, buttery chicory is one of my favourite things to eat. This makes a tasty lunch or light supper and is a good accompaniment to steak.**

1. Preheat the oven to 220°C.

2. Trim any damaged or wilted outside leaves from the chicory. Trim a sliver off the root, making sure all the leaves are still attached, and cut each head in half through the root.

3. Dry-fry the bacon in a frying or sauté pan, large enough to hold the chicory halves in one layer, until golden and crisp. Remove with a slotted spoon and set aside.

4. Melt the butter in the unwashed bacon pan. Sprinkle the cut sides of the chicory with salt and place cut-side down in the pan. Cook slowly over a low to medium heat for 5–10 minutes or until golden brown. The aim is for the chicory to be cooked by the time it becomes golden brown. Add a splash of water if it is browning too quickly. Turn it over when golden and cook for a few more minutes. Transfer to a shallow ovenproof baking dish and scatter with the bacon, crumbled cheese and walnuts.

5. Bake in the preheated oven for 5–10 minutes, or until golden and the cheese has melted. Season and finish with a swirl of walnut oil, if using, and some parsley.

### Get Ahead

Make to the end of step 4 up to 3 days in advance and keep in the fridge, covered.

### Hints & Tips

Step 5 can be omitted altogether. Simply serve the chicory straightaway on individual plates, or on one pretty dish or plate, topped with the bacon, crumbled cheese, roughly chopped walnuts, parsley and walnut oil, if using. I often take this route – it's just as good either way!

# TOMATO, KALE & ANCHOVY GNOCCHI

SERVES 2–3

**olive oil**
**400g (14oz) tin of chopped tomatoes**
**a pinch of sugar**
**a good pinch of dried oregano**
**200g (7oz) kale (or cavolo nero or chard)**
**6 anchovies (optional)**
**1 clove of garlic, crushed**
**200g (7oz) fresh potato gnocchi**
**a little grated Parmesan cheese**
**salt and freshly ground black pepper**

### Hints & Tips

- If using prepared kale, pick over and discard the tough stems and spiny bits. For unprepared kale or cavolo nero, strip out any older, fatter stems from the leaves and discard. Stack the leaves into piles, roll them up into fat cigarettes and cut across into 2cm- (¾in-) wide ribbons. Wash before using.
- Delicious in its own right, this is ideal for vegetarians if you leave out the anchovies and use a vegetarian alternative to Parmesan, and also very good as an accompaniment to chicken and fish.

**A quick lunch or supper that's bursting with flavour. Gnocchi take only a minute or two to cook and, very helpfully, bob up to the top of the pan when ready. Use chard or cavolo nero instead of kale, if you have it. Fresh gnocchi are available alongside fresh pasta in most supermarkets.**

1. Heat a little olive oil in a saucepan, add the tomatoes, sugar and oregano, plus a little salt and pepper, and bubble until the runny liquid has reduced and the tomatoes have formed a thickish sauce. Check the seasoning and set aside.

2. Meanwhile, cook the kale in a large pan of boiling salted water for a few minutes, until just cooked. Drain and refresh under cold water to stop it cooking and to set the colour. Gently squeeze out the excess water using your hands.

3. Put a large pan of salted water on to boil for the gnocchi.

4. Heat a tablespoon of olive oil in the unwashed kale saucepan and, with scissors, snip the anchovies, if using, into the pan. Stir for a minute or so until they have melted into the oil (a few lumps are fine). Add the garlic and stir for a minute, then add the kale, followed by the tomato sauce.

5. Tip the gnocchi into the boiling water and cook for a few minutes until they rise to the top. Drain immediately and gently stir into the tomato and kale mixture. Tip into a serving dish, or bowls, and scatter with grated Parmesan cheese.

### Get Ahead

Steps 1, 2 and 4 can be prepared up to a day ahead. Reheat the sauce before adding the cooked gnocchi.

# BEETROOT & FENNEL-CURED SALMON

SERVES 6 FOR LUNCH
OR 8–12 AS A STARTER

**800–900g (1¾–2lb) piece of salmon fillet, skinned**
**2 level tbsp granulated sugar**
**2 level tbsp sea salt**
**1 tbsp fennel seeds, roughly crushed**
**2 medium raw beetroots (approximately 300g/11oz), peeled and grated**
**See below for sauces and serving suggestions**

### Get Ahead

- This will keep for a week in the fridge. It also freezes beautifully and can even be sliced from frozen.
- Slice up to 24 hours ahead, re-form and keep in the fridge, tightly wrapped in clingfilm. At any time on the day of serving, arrange on the serving plate(s), cover with clingfilm, stack and store in the fridge until required.
- The sauces and cucumber ribbons can be made up to 24 hours in advance.

### Hints & Tips

- Very good with griddled bread (see Roast Bone Marrow, page 22).
- For canapés, spread a slice of salmon with a little plain horseradish sauce, put a strip of cucumber on top and roll up. Secure with a cocktail stick, if you like, and serve standing up with a little dill or parsley poking out of the top. These can be made up to 24 hours ahead, but top with the herbs on the day.

**The sweet, earthy flavour of beetroot marries beautifully with salmon and they look very pretty together. Serve with new potatoes for a delicious lunch or light supper, with griddled bread as a starter or as get-ahead canapés (see Hints & Tips, below left). I grate the beetroot in a processor, but still advise wearing gloves!**

1. Run your fingers over the salmon and remove any remaining pin bones.

2. Combine the sugar, salt, fennel seeds and beetroot together in a bowl. Lay out a very large piece of clingfilm (it needs to be more than twice the size of the piece of salmon) and spread half the beetroot mixture, roughly the same size as the salmon, in the middle. Place the salmon skinned-side down on top and cover with the rest of the beetroot mixture. Wrap the clingfilm around the salmon, leaving all the seams uppermost. Put onto a flat plate or tray (with a lip, to catch the juices that will seep out), cover with a board or flat tray and weigh down lightly using weights or tins. Leave at room temperature for an hour or two, then refrigerate for 24 hours, after which the salmon colour will still be visible in the middle, or 36–48 hours for beetroot-coloured slices.

3. Remove the clingfilm, drain off the liquid and discard the beetroot. Rinse and dry the salmon. Wrap in fresh clingfilm and refrigerate until required.

4. To serve, slice the fish very thinly, starting from the tail end. Arrange on a large platter or individual plates and serve with any of the sauces and accompaniments below.

## HORSERADISH SAUCE

Mix 3 tbsp horseradish sauce, 2 tbsp freshly chopped dill and some seasoning into a 200g (7oz) carton of crème fraîche. Or substitute seedy and/or Dijon mustard for the horseradish.

## CUCUMBER & DILL SAUCE

Peel and shave a cucumber into long ribbons using a potato peeler, discarding the core of pips. Snip the strips into smaller chunks, put into a sieve, sprinkle with salt and leave to drain for 30 minutes. Squeeze out the excess liquid, and mix with 200g (7oz) crème fraîche, 2 tbsp freshly chopped dill, 2 sliced spring onions and seasoning. Add a crushed clove of garlic for some extra zing.

## CUCUMBER RIBBONS WITH FENNEL SHAVINGS

Prepare a cucumber as for the sauce above and drain for 30 minutes (this can be done up to 24 hours ahead). Before serving, mix with shavings of raw fennel, a grinding of black pepper, a spritz of lemon juice and a few dill or fennel fronds.

# VIETNAMESE PRAWN ROLLS

MAKES 12–14 ROLLS

**12–14 round 16cm (6½in) rice wrappers (banh trang)**

FOR THE DIPPING SAUCE

**1 tbsp sugar**
**2 tbsp fish sauce**
**2 tbsp freshly squeezed lime juice (1 juicy lime)**
**1 large clove of garlic, chopped**
**1 red chilli, chopped**

FOR THE FILLING

**a small bunch of coriander**
**¼ cucumber, cut into thin matchsticks**
**400g (14oz) frozen, cooked, peeled prawns, thawed and very well drained**
**4 spring onions, trimmed and finely sliced lengthways**
**bean sprouts (optional)**
**mint leaves**
**salted peanuts, roughly chopped**
**chives (optional)**

### Get Ahead

Make the rolls up to 24 hours in advance and the sauce several days in advance.

**Fresh and summery, light and healthy, fat-free and crunchy, with a tangy sweet, sour, spicy and salty dipping sauce. These make delicious do-ahead canapés, too, and are far easier to make than you might think. No cooking required!**

1. Make the dipping sauce by mixing all the ingredients together. Set aside.

2. Wet two scrunched-up pieces of kitchen paper, squeeze out the excess water and spread one out on a worktop and line a plate with the other.

3. Dip a rice wrapper into a bowl of warm water for 1 second – in and out – then spread it out on the kitchen paper on the worktop.

4. Spread a row of coriander along the middle of the wrapper, top with some cucumber, prawns, spring onions and bean sprouts, if using. Finally, arrange a row of mint leaves over the top. *Wet your fingers*, roll up tightly and put seam-side down on the lined plate. Continue with the rest of the wrappers. If not using immediately, cover with another piece of damp kitchen paper and clingfilm and refrigerate.

5. To serve, either cut each roll into four pieces and arrange six of these standing up on individual plates, or cut each one in half on a deep diagonal and arrange three of these propped up artistically against each other on individual plates.

6. Just before serving, spoon over a *little* of the sauce (not much, as a little goes a long way!) and garnish with chopped peanuts and sprigs of coriander and/or chives.

### Hints & Tips

- All quantities are approximate as it depends what and how much you put into each roll.
- Only make one roll at a time. Water is the answer to everything as it stops the wrappers from sticking and also acts as glue when rolling up. If a wrapper is too sticky, floppy or soft, discard it – it's been soaked for too long. Don't worry if one breaks and falls apart – simply start again with a new wrapper (there are more than 100 wrappers in a 400g/14oz pack).
- The rolls look good with a chive sticking out at either end, which needs to be incorporated while rolling.
- Cut the rolls into four and serve as canapés, standing up, with a chive or other herb sticking out of the top.
- Other filling ideas include shredded chicken, duck, pork, lettuce, crab and rice noodles.

# CELERY & BLUE CHEESE SOUP WITH BLUE CHEESE & WALNUT RAREBITS

Ⓥ

SERVES 4–6

**1 head of celery**
**olive oil**
**a knob of butter**
**1 large onion, roughly chopped**
**1 heaped tbsp flour (or 1 medium potato, sliced)**
**850ml (1½ pint) vegetable or chicken stock (or 2 stock cubes)**
**55g (2oz) blue cheese, broken into rough chunks**
**a grating of nutmeg**
**4 tbsp cream (optional)**
**salt and freshly ground black pepper**

SERVING SUGGESTIONS
**Celery leaves, chopped parsley or chives, roughly chopped walnuts, cream, crispy bacon or pancetta, grated nutmeg**

**Get Ahead**
The soup will sit happily in the fridge for 4 days. It also freezes beautifully.

**Hints & Tips**
- For gluten-free soup, use a potato to thicken the soup instead of flour.
- When reheating the soup, bring to just below boiling point – don't let it boil.

**A comforting and warming meal in itself, and a good way of using up leftover blue cheese.**

1. Cut the root off the celery, wash the sticks and chop into chunks, leaves and all. (You may like to reserve a few leaves for decoration.)

2. Heat a little olive oil and a small knob of butter in a saucepan, add the celery and onion, cover with a lid and cook very gently for about 10 minutes, until soft but not coloured.

3. Stir in the flour and add the stock (or stock cubes and water). Bring to the boil, season and simmer for 20 minutes, or until the celery is very soft.

4. Liquidize the soup, adding the blue cheese to the liquidizer at the same time. Sieve and thin with a little water or stock if it's too thick. Add a grating of nutmeg (or a pinch of ground nutmeg) and check the seasoning. Stir in the cream, if using, and serve with Blue Cheese & Walnut Rarebits (see below).

## BLUE CHEESE & WALNUT RAREBITS

MAKES 8

**1 ciabatta loaf**
**110g (4oz) creamy blue cheese**
**1 egg white**
**a few walnuts, roughly chopped**

1. Preheat the oven to 220°C, or turn on the grill to its highest setting.

2. Cut eight diagonal slices, about 1cm (½in) thick, from the ciabatta loaf and spread these croûtes on a baking sheet.

3. In a small bowl, break up the cheese with a fork until paste-like. Gradually add the egg white, bit by bit, beating with the fork or a small whisk between each addition. There will be a few lumps, which don't matter at all. The mixture should be of spreadable consistency and quite loose, but not so loose that it runs over the edges of the croûtes. You may not need all the egg white. Stir in the chopped walnuts.

4. Spread the cheese mixture over the croûtes, right to the edges. Cook in the preheated oven, or under the grill, for 6–10 minutes, or until golden brown and bubbling. Serve with the soup.

**Get Ahead**
Prepare the rarebits to the end of step 3 up to 3 days in advance.

**Hints & Tips**
In miniature, these make very tasty canapés, or just cut the croûtes into thin strips. A very good savoury, too.

# SALMON & PRAWN BRIOCHE BURGERS WITH WATERCRESS, LIME & WASABI MAYO

MAKES 4–6

500g (1lb 2oz) salmon fillet, skinless
350g (12oz) frozen cooked prawns, thawed, drained and dried (225g/8oz thawed weight)
4 spring onions, trimmed and roughly chopped
2.5cm (1in) piece of ginger, peeled and roughly chopped quite small (or ready-prepared from a jar)
olive oil
4–6 brioche burger buns, halved
crisp lettuce leaves
½ a small red onion, very thinly sliced (you won't need it all)
4–6 large shell-on cooked prawns (optional)
salt and freshly ground black pepper

FOR THE WATERCRESS, LIME & WASABI MAYONNAISE
6 tbsp mayonnaise
2 good handfuls of watercress
2 tsp wasabi paste
freshly squeezed juice of ½ a lime

**Burgers hardly need introduction, however these are healthier than most, yet no less tasty for it! Very good without the bun, too, with salad and a salsa.**

1. Cut 300g (10oz) of the salmon into chunks and process briefly with roughly half of the prawns, the spring onions, ginger and some seasoning, just until it becomes paste-like. Scrape into a bowl. Cut the remaining salmon into 1cm (½in) dice and stir into the salmon mixture. Check the seasoning. Shape into four large or six smaller burgers and set aside.

2. Process the mayonnaise, watercress and wasabi paste together, then add the lime juice. Check the seasoning and set aside.

3. Heat a frying pan with a little olive oil, and fry the burgers for 2–3 minutes on each side, depending on their thickness, until a golden crust has formed. They should still be slightly undercooked in the middle. Alternatively, heat a griddle pan until very hot, brush the burgers with a little oil and cook as above. Meanwhile, lightly toast the buns, being careful not to burn them as the brioche contains sugar.

4. Spread both halves of each bun with the wasabi mayo. Arrange lettuce leaves on each base, followed by the burgers, a dollop of the mayo, red onion slices, the reserved prawns and then the lid of the bun. Finally, if using, sit a large prawn on top and secure in place with a cocktail stick.

**Get Ahead**
Make steps 1–2 up to 24 hours ahead, cover and refrigerate.

**Hints & Tips**
The mayonnaise is beyond delicious spooned over halved, 6-minute-boiled eggs, sitting atop toasted sourdough bread. A slice or two of smoked salmon alongside transforms this into a delectable starter or lunch.

# CRISPY LAMB FILO ROLLS WITH HARISSA YOGHURT

MAKES 12

olive oil
1 onion, finely chopped
1½ tsp garam masala
1 tsp ground cumin
1 tsp ground cinnamon
a pinch of chilli powder
1 tsp salt and freshly ground black pepper
450g (1lb) cooked or uncooked lamb, minced
2 tbsp barberries, raisins or sultanas
2 good handfuls of frozen peas
2 tbsp pine nuts, toasted
55g (2oz) butter, melted
3 sheets of filo pastry (see Hints & Tips, below right)
nigella seeds

FOR THE SAUCE
200g (7oz) natural yoghurt
1 tsp harissa paste, plus a little extra
salt
a few fresh mint leaves

### Get Ahead

- Make to the end of step 4 up to 2 days in advance and refrigerate, or freeze. Bring back to room temperature for an hour or so, or thaw for 2–3 hours, before cooking.
- The sauce can be made up to 3 days in advance, but leave the mint until serving.

**A tasty way of using up leftover lamb, but equally good with fresh lamb mince, these rolls are easier to make than they look and are a lovely get-ahead lunch or supper. Great with Kisir (see page 148), Fattoush (see page 154) or a green salad.**

1. Heat a little olive oil in a frying pan, add the onion and cook until soft. Add the spices, salt and pepper, and cook for a minute or two until it becomes fragrant. If using cooked lamb mince, add it and cook, while stirring, for a few minutes. If using uncooked mince, cook for 5 minutes more. Stir in the barberries, raisins or sultanas, the peas and pine nuts. Set aside to cool.

2. Line a baking sheet with silicone paper, or brush with some of the melted butter.

3. Unwrap the pastry, peel off one sheet and cover the remainder with a damp cloth. Lay it out horizontally and brush with butter. Cut into four long, narrow, equal-sized rectangles by making three parallel cuts from one short edge of the pastry to the other short edge.

4. Put a heaped tablespoon of the lamb mixture along the bottom end of each rectangle, and roll up quite tightly into a sausage shape. A few escaped bits are inevitable, but just shove them back in. Roughly pinch the ends together, like a cracker. Put onto the baking sheet, seam-side down, and repeat with the rest of the pastry and mixture. Brush the rolls with melted butter and sprinkle with nigella seeds. Cover lightly with clingfilm until required.

5. For the sauce, mix the yoghurt and harissa paste together and season well with salt. Put into a small serving bowl and swirl a little extra harissa paste over the top. Scatter with a few roughly chopped mint leaves and set aside.

6. Preheat the oven to 200°C. Cook the rolls for 10–15 minutes or until golden brown and crispy. Serve cut in half diagonally and propped up on each other, pointed end uppermost, with the sauce on the side.

### Hints & Tips

- I use filo pastry sheets measuring 46 x 25cm (18 x 10in), but the size can vary according to the brand. You can make the rolls fuller, thinner, longer or shorter, according to the pastry you use, or form into triangles.
- The rolls are filling, so one would be plenty for light eaters.
- **Other ideas for using the spiced lamb:** Spread hummus over flatbreads, chapattis or tortillas, top with the lamb, a few chickpeas, yoghurt, sumac, pomegranate seeds and mint. Or stuff into pitta pockets with shredded lettuce, sliced red onion, mint and yoghurt, or minty mayo.

# EASY SUPPERS & COMFORTING FOOD

# SPINACH, MUSHROOM & TALEGGIO GALETTE

SERVES 5–6

**350g (12oz) mixed mushrooms**
**a good knob of butter**
**1 clove garlic, crushed**
**a little grated nutmeg**
**500g (1lb 2oz) fresh spinach**
**1 heaped tsp Dijon mustard**
**200ml (7fl oz) crème fraîche**
**½ a 500g (1lb 2oz) block of shortcrust pastry (or see Hints & Tips, below)**
**a few sprigs (4–6) of fresh thyme, or 1–2 tsp dried**
**1 egg**
**85g (3oz) Taleggio cheese, straight from the fridge**
**nigella seeds and fresh thyme sprigs, to garnish**
**salt and freshly ground black pepper**

### Get Ahead

Make to the end of step 5 up to 24 hours ahead, cover and refrigerate. Bring back to room temperature an hour or so before cooking. Or, prepare steps 1 and 2 up to 3 days in advance and store as above.

### Hints & Tips

- Instead of using a block of pastry, you can use a round disc of ready-rolled shortcrust pastry.
- Chard or kale are delicious alternatives to spinach. Chicken, bacon, ham and smoked fish all make good additions, too.

**Rustic, super-savoury, very easy and very delicious! Cheesy, thyme pastry filled with an oozing, creamy filling.**

**1.** Slice any large mushrooms into thick slices, halve medium-sized ones and leave smaller ones whole. Melt the butter in a frying pan, add the mushrooms and plenty of seasoning, and cook over a high heat until they are dry, sizzling and beginning to brown around the edges. Add the garlic and nutmeg, and cook for a further minute. Spread onto a plate to cool.

**2.** While the mushrooms are cooking, wilt the spinach with a little salt and a dribble of water in a dry saucepan, or use a microwave. Either way, it will only take a few minutes. Drain, cool under cold water and squeeze out *all* the moisture in batches with your hands. Put into a bowl and mix with the mushrooms. Mix the mustard, crème fraîche and some salt and black pepper together in the crème fraîche carton. Check the seasoning and incorporate into the spinach and mushroom mixture.

**3.** Preheat the oven to 200°C and put in a flat baking sheet to warm.

**4.** Roll the pastry roughly into a circle, about 38cm (15in) across, and scatter with fresh thyme sprigs (if the stems are soft, or just the leaves if not) or dried thyme. Gently roll the thyme into the pastry. Transfer onto a sheet of silicone or baking paper.

**5.** Spoon the filling into the middle of the pastry, aiming for a bit of height, leaving a 5cm (2in) rim around the edges. Bring the edge of the pastry up over the outside of the filling, leaving most of the filling showing, and pleat the pastry to form a wavy effect around the rim. It's meant to look rustic and needs a bit of height to hold the filling in while cooking, although any leakages are tasty additions to the rustic charm.

**6.** Using a fork, lightly beat the egg with a pinch of salt, then brush the pleated pastry rim with the egg wash. Thinly slice the cheese and dot over both the filling and the pastry rims. Scatter with some nigella seeds and a few sprigs of thyme (or a sprinkling of dried).

**7.** Remove the baking sheet from the oven, carefully slide the galette onto it and cook for 20–25 minutes, or until golden brown and bubbling. Leave for a few minutes before transferring to a serving platter or board, and a few more minutes before eating – if it's steaming hot, it will taste of nothing.

# TURKISH LAMB MEATBALLS WITH BULGUR PILAF

SERVES 4 (MAKES 14–16 MEATBALLS)

500g (1lb 2oz) minced lamb, as lean as possible
1 clove of garlic, crushed
5 spring onions, chopped
2 tsp ground coriander
1 tsp ground cumin
1 tsp salt
½ tsp ground cinnamon
a pinch of chilli powder
1 tsp ginger, grated (or ready-prepared from a jar)
1 tbsp freshly chopped mint, plus a little extra for serving
1 tbsp freshly chopped parsley
1 egg, beaten, to bind
vegetable oil

FOR THE SAUCE
400g (14oz) tin of chopped tomatoes
½ tsp ground cinnamon
a pinch of sugar
1 tsp salt and ground black pepper

FOR THE PILAF
30g (1oz) butter
100g (3½oz) orzo
200g (7oz) bulgur wheat
1 tsp ground cumin
1 heaped tsp salt
a bunch of dill, chopped (optional)
salt and freshly ground black pepper

SERVING SUGGESTIONS
Greek yoghurt, pomegranate seeds, dried cranberries or barberries, dried rose petals, chopped mint or parsley, naan or other flatbreads

**An easy supper that lends itself to relaxed entertaining, too. The pilaf has a lovely, deep buttery flavour, is delicious as an accompaniment to so many things, and as a main course in its own right with almost anything added to it.**

**1.** Mix all the meatball ingredients, except the egg and vegetable oil, together well – using your hands is best! Add a little egg, just to bind the mixture – you may not need it all; be careful not to make the mixture too wet. With wet hands, shape into 14–16 balls, the size of golf balls.

**2.** Heat a little oil in a sauté or frying pan and add the meatballs. Fry, turning, until the meatballs are golden brown all over. Pour off all but 1 tbsp of fat. Add all the sauce ingredients, rinse out the tomato tin with a little water and add, then cover and simmer for 10–15 minutes, turning once.

**3.** Meanwhile, for the pilaf, melt the butter in a lidded saucepan. Add the orzo and stir over the heat for a few minutes until golden brown. Add the bulgur wheat and continue to stir for a further 2 minutes. Stir in the cumin, salt and pepper.

**4.** Add 425ml (15fl oz) water to the pilaf, bring to the boil, cover and cook on the lowest heat for 10 minutes, until all the liquid has been absorbed. Remove from the heat and take off the lid, cover with a tea towel or cloth, replace the lid and leave to steam for 10 minutes. Fork up, check the seasoning and add the dill, if using.

**5.** Garnish the meatballs (see the suggestions, left) and serve with the pilaf.

### Get Ahead

- This recipe can be made up to 3 days in advance. Reheat the meatballs and decorate when required. They can be frozen before or after cooking.
- **Reheating the pilaf:**
  **Microwave:** 1–2 minutes in a shallow dish, splashed with a little water.
  **Saucepan or sauté pan:** Heat a little oil, butter or a splash of water, add the pilaf and stir with a wooden spoon for a few minutes until hot.
  **Oven:** 150°C in a shallow ovenproof dish with a splash of water, covered with a lid or foil, for around 15 minutes, stirring halfway through.

### Hints & Tips

- Shaped into oval kofte kebabs and then grilled, barbecued or fried, the lamb is delicious stuffed into pitta pockets or other flatbreads or wraps, with feta cheese, sliced red onion, tomatoes, chilli, yoghurt, parsley and/or mint – and anything else fresh and crunchy.
- Many things can be added to transform the pilaf from an accompaniment to a main course or salad, eaten warm or cold – for example, cooked chicken, meat, dried cranberries, barberries, nuts, seeds, vegetables, herbs and spices.

# BAKED MEDITERRANEAN FISH

SERVES 4

55g (2oz) stoned black olives, roughly chopped
6 anchovies, chopped
1 tbsp capers
4 tbsp sun-dried tomato purée or paste
1 tbsp olive oil
4 x 140g (5oz) fillets of white fish, such as haddock or cod
fresh basil leaves

**Recipes don't get much easier or quicker than this lovely, healthy supper. Simplicity itself!**

1. Preheat the oven to 200°C. Line a baking sheet with greased foil or silicone paper.

2. In a bowl, mix together all the ingredients except for the fish and basil leaves.

3. Cut the fillets in half to form two triangular shapes, tucking the thin tail ends underneath to create a more even thickness. Place on the lined baking sheet, divide the olive mixture between them and spread evenly over the top.

4. Bake in the preheated oven for 5–6 minutes, depending on the thickness of the fillets. Serve immediately with a swirl of olive oil and a basil leaf or two on top of each fillet.

### Get Ahead

Make the topping up to 3 days ahead and keep in the fridge, covered.

### Hints & Tips

Fish loins, rather than fillets, are thicker and won't need to be cut in half. They will take a few minutes longer to cook.

# SMOKED HADDOCK, LEEK & ORZO GRATIN

SERVES 5–6

**A winter warmer in every sense – comforting and extremely tasty. Very creamy, too, yet with the addition of hardly any cream. Easy and incredibly quick to rustle up, this is a variation on fish pie and it takes less than half the time to make. One of my all-time most popular recipes.**

olive oil
1 medium onion, finely chopped
1 large leek, sliced
300g (11oz) orzo
1 litre (1¾ pints) fish or chicken stock (or 2 stock cubes)
2 fillets of undyed smoked haddock, roughly 340g (12oz), skinned
200g (7oz) Taleggio cheese, chopped into 1cm (½in) dice
4–5 tbsp double cream
2–3 tbsp grated Parmesan cheese
2–3 tbsp dried breadcrumbs
chopped parsley (optional)
salt and freshly ground black pepper

**1.** Preheat the oven to 220°C.

**2.** Heat a little oil in a large saucepan, add the onion and leek and cook gently until softened.

**3.** Add the orzo and stir to coat in the oil. Add the stock and bring to the boil. Check and adjust the seasoning. Simmer for 9 minutes, until the pasta is just cooked. The mixture will be fairly sloppy, which is good.

**4.** While the pasta is cooking, cut the smoked haddock into fairly small dice (I use scissors). Remove the orzo mixture from the heat and gently stir in the smoked haddock, the chunks of Taleggio and the cream. Check the seasoning. Tip into a shallow ovenproof dish and sprinkle with the Parmesan and a few dried breadcrumbs.

**5.** Bake in the preheated oven for 15–20 minutes or until golden brown and bubbling. Scatter with chopped parsley, if using, and serve with a green salad or some plain green vegetables.

### Get Ahead

Prepare to the end of step 4 up to 2 days in advance. Cool, cover and refrigerate, or freeze. Bring back to room temperature before baking.

### Hints & Tips

- Smoked mackerel is a delicious substitute for the haddock, as is cooked chicken, turkey, ham or bacon. Taleggio can be replaced with pretty much any creamy cheese.
- Any leftovers are super-delicious when topped with a fried or poached egg – as are most things!

# HADDOCK FISHCAKES WITH WATERCRESS SAUCE & CRISPY FRIED PARSLEY

MAKES 8

500g (1lb 2oz) potatoes, peeled
30g (1oz) butter, plus extra for frying
250g (9oz) fresh haddock
250g (9oz) undyed smoked haddock
150ml (5fl oz) milk
1 tbsp anchovy essence or paste
1 tbsp small capers
2 tbsp freshly chopped parsley, plus a good handful of curly-leaf parsley sprigs for frying
flour, for coating
olive oil
1 lemon, cut into wedges
salt and freshly ground black pepper

FOR THE WATERCRESS SAUCE

1 bag of watercress (approximately 85g/3oz)
150ml (5fl oz) crème fraîche
freshly squeezed lemon juice, to taste

**Get Ahead**

- Make to the end of step 3 up to 3 days ahead. Cover and chill.
- Make step 4 up to 24 hours ahead and chill, covered, in a bowl. Do not heat the sauce until required, as this will impair the bright green colour.

**Not exactly reinventing the wheel, nor are these fine dining, but they are filling, comforting and especially useful if you have leftover mash. We always had crispy fried parsley with fish when I was growing up, and how very tasty it is. An easy make-ahead lunch or supper.**

**1.** Cut the potatoes into even-sized pieces, bring to the boil in a pan of cold salted water and simmer until cooked. Drain, allow the steam to subside for a few minutes, then mash with the butter and plenty of seasoning.

**2.** Meanwhile, put all the fish into a saucepan, snipping the fillets into pieces if necessary. Pour over the milk to barely cover, bring slowly to the boil, remove from the heat and set aside for a few minutes. Drain, discarding the milk.

**3.** In a large bowl, mix together the mashed potato, haddock, broken into large flakes, anchovy essence, capers and chopped parsley. Check the seasoning and add more salt or anchovy essence, as required – it should be well seasoned. Divide the mixture into 8. Spread a little flour onto a plate and your hands. Mould the mixture into 8 fishcakes by rolling it into a ball between your palms and then flattening it into cakes. Lightly coat in the flour. Transfer to a plate or tray lined with clingfilm, cover and put in the fridge for about 30 minutes to firm up.

**4.** Meanwhile, for the sauce, blitz the watercress and crème fraîche together using an electric hand-held wand or a small processor or grinder. Check the seasoning and set aside in a saucepan.

**5.** Heat a little oil, butter and a sprinkling of salt in a frying pan, and cook the fishcakes for 3–4 minutes on each side, or until golden brown. Allow a good, thick crust to form on the bottom before turning, or the base will be left stuck to the pan. To avoid overcrowding the pan, you may need to do this in batches.

**6.** Add a little more oil to the pan, if necessary, and stir-fry the sprigs of parsley for a few minutes. They will spit! Drain on kitchen paper and sprinkle with salt. They will crisp up as they cool.

**7.** Gently heat the sauce, thinning it with a tablespoon of water, if necessary, and adding lemon juice to taste. Serve the fishcakes topped with fried parsley, the watercress sauce and wedges of lemon.

# ONE-PAN COD, CHORIZO & CHICKPEAS

SERVES 4

13cm (5in) piece of chorizo, halved lengthways and sliced into 5mm- (¼in-) thick half-moons
2 cloves of garlic, crushed
a good pinch of dried oregano
1 tsp rose harissa paste, plus a little extra for serving
400g (14oz) tin of chickpeas, drained and rinsed
400g (14oz) tin of chopped tomatoes
½ tsp sugar
4 x fillets of cod (total weight approximately 550g/1lb 4oz)
olive oil
100g (3½oz) samphire (optional)
salt and freshly ground black pepper

TO SERVE

Yoghurt, harissa paste, roughly chopped fresh soft green herbs, bread for mopping

**We eat this tasty, easy, very healthy and quick supper, which takes no more than 20 minutes from start to finish, most weeks. We're lucky enough to have a fishmonger who calls in his van every Thursday with fish so fresh it's squeaky, whiter than white and odourless – exactly as fish should be. I've suggested using cod here, but almost any other white fish would work just as well.**

**1.** Cook the chorizo in a dry sauté or frying pan (preferably one that has a lid) for 2–3 minutes, until the oil begins to run. Add the garlic and oregano and stir for a minute. Add the harissa paste, chickpeas, tomatoes and sugar, and season well. Bring to the boil and simmer gently for 5 minutes.

**2.** Cut the fish fillets into halves or thirds, depending on their size, and tuck the thinner ends under to make them an even thickness. Sit the fish on top of the chickpea mixture in one layer, sprinkle with a little salt and olive oil, cover with the lid or some foil, bring back to the boil and simmer gently for 5 minutes, or until the fish has turned opaque and is just cooked.

**3.** Meanwhile, if using, cook the samphire for 3 minutes in boiling water and drain.

**4.** Remove the lid from the fish, blob with yoghurt and swirl a little harissa paste into it. Top with the samphire, if using, and the chopped herbs, and serve straight from the pan, with bread to mop up the juices.

### Get Ahead

Cook to the end of step 1 up to 2 days in advance. The fish can also be prepared up to 24 hours in advance.

### Hints & Tips

- Stir a few handfuls of fresh spinach or cooked chard into the chickpea mixture just before putting the fish on top.
- Substitute eggs for the fish – make little hollows in the chickpea mixture, break eggs into them, season, cover and cook the same way as above until the whites are just set.

# SLOW-BRAISED BEEF SHORT RIBS WITH HORSERADISH CREAM

SERVES 4

4 short ribs of beef (see Hints & Tips, below)
1 tbsp seasoned flour
vegetable oil
1 onion, sliced
1 parsnip, peeled and diced
2 cloves of garlic, crushed
300ml (10fl oz) red wine
500ml (18fl oz) beef stock (or use 1 stock cube)
1 tbsp sun-dried tomato paste or tomato purée
a good pinch of dried thyme
2 bay leaves
salt and freshly ground black pepper

FOR THE HORSERADISH CREAM
110g (4oz) crème fraîche
2 tsp creamed horseradish
1 tsp English mustard
1 tbsp chopped chives

### Get Ahead

The ribs and sauce can be made up to 4 days in advance. The ribs also freeze well.

**This flavourful meat is cooked slowly until succulent and falling off the bone into its dark, deeply rich sauce. Serve with creamy mashed potatoes and earthy vegetables, such as cabbage, chard, kale, celeriac purée (see page 110) or leeks in white sauce. This is best started at least a day before eating.**

**1.** Preheat the oven to 170°C.

**2.** Trim the ribs of all excess fat and toss in the seasoned flour until coated all over. Heat a little oil in a casserole or saucepan and brown the ribs well on all sides, in batches if necessary.

**3.** Remove from the pan and drain off all but 1–2 tablespoons of fat, or add a little more oil to the pan if necessary. Cook the onion and parsnip, stirring occasionally, until beginning to brown. This is important, as it will give the sauce a good colour and flavour. Add the garlic and cook for a further minute.

**4.** Return the ribs to the pan, with the bones uppermost if possible, and add the rest of the ingredients. Bring to the boil and check the seasoning (it will taste rather raw and bitter at this stage because of the uncooked wine).

**5.** Transfer to the preheated oven and cook for 3 hours, or until the meat is almost falling off the bones, giving it a gentle stir roughly halfway through and adding a little more liquid if necessary.

**6.** Meanwhile, mix together the horseradish cream ingredients, leaving a few chives aside for garnishing. Season with salt and pepper and loosen with a little water if necessary.

**7.** Skim the fat from the top of the casserole if eating straightaway or, better still, cool, cover and refrigerate overnight. Lift off and discard the layer of fat that has set on the top. Reheat on the hob or in a medium oven for 20–30 minutes when required.

**8.** Serve on a platter with the horseradish cream dribbled over the top and the reserved chives.

### Hints & Tips

- The ribs are available from good supermarkets, or ask the butcher for beef short ribs (or thin ribs, or Jacob's Ladder), roughly 10 x 6cm (4 x 2½in) or half a rib.
- If the sauce is too runny, remove the ribs and bubble it furiously for 10 minutes or so, until it has thickened to your liking.

# DUKKAH-CRUSTED CHICKEN THIGH FILLETS WITH LIME YOGHURT & POMEGRANATE

SERVES 4

8 boneless, skinless chicken thigh fillets, well trimmed
200g (7oz) natural yoghurt
1 lime
salt
2 tbsp pomegranate seeds
a few sprigs of coriander or parsley, roughly chopped

FOR THE MARINADE
1 tsp ground cinnamon
1 tsp turmeric
6 tsp dukkah
4 tbsp vegetable oil

**When short of time, this is the recipe I turn to for an easy tasty supper. Eat this with almost any grain or warm flatbread. A fresh crisp salad of chunkily chopped tomatoes, cucumber and onion, perhaps with a hint of chilli, would be good, too, or a green veg. Omit the lime if you don't have one to hand.**

**1.** Snip a cut of approximately 1cm (½in) through the membrane and flesh on both sides of each thigh, to stop them curling up when cooking.

**2.** Mix the marinade ingredients together. Add the chicken and coat well. Marinate for up to 24 hours – this isn't vital.

**3.** Mix the yoghurt with the juice from half the lime and season with salt. Set aside.

**4.** Heat a frying or griddle pan until hot. Sprinkle the skinned side of the chicken with salt and cook, salted-side down and opened out flat, in the dry pan. Press down with a fish slice then fry until crisp and golden. Sprinkle with salt, turn them over and repeat, until the chicken is cooked through. This will take 5–6 minutes on each side. If you need to cook in batches, wipe out the pan in between.

**5.** Top each thigh with a dollop of yoghurt sauce (serve the rest separately), scatter with the pomegranate seeds and roughly chopped herbs, and squeeze over the remaining lime.

### Get Ahead

Prepare steps 1–3 up to 24 hours in advance.

### Hints & Tips

I would choose chicken thighs over breasts any day as they are far more succulent and juicy, considerably cheaper and hard to overcook.

# ALL-IN-ONE CHORIZO CHICKEN

SERVES 4

olive oil
750g (1lb 10oz) waxy new potatoes, cut into 3 or 4 slices lengthways, depending on size
a good pinch of dried oregano
1 head of garlic, cloves peeled
150g (5½oz) piece of chorizo (soft salami-style), skinned, halved lengthways and sliced a bit thicker than a £1 coin
8 chicken thighs, skin-on and bone-in, very well trimmed of all visible fat
1–2 tsp hot smoked paprika
a good handful of pitted black olives
a little freshly chopped parsley
salt and freshly ground black pepper

**Easy, quick to prepare and inexpensive, this is a delicious Spanish-influenced supper or lunch. The lovely red-orange spices and flavours from the chorizo permeate the potatoes underneath during cooking, while the chicken gets nice and crispy on top.**

**1.** Preheat the oven to 220°C. Lightly oil a large shallow roasting tin or ovenproof dish. It needs to be big enough to hold the potatoes in one layer and with a little space around each thigh.

**2.** Spread the potatoes out over the tin, season, sprinkle with some oregano and nestle in the garlic cloves. Scatter over the chorizo and sit the chicken thighs on top (they shouldn't be touching).

**3.** Sprinkle everything with the smoked paprika and some seasoning, trickle over a dash of olive oil and bake at the top of the oven for 30 minutes. Baste with the juices; turn over any charred pieces of chorizo, scatter over the black olives and return to the oven for another 15 minutes or until cooked through (larger thighs may take a little longer). Turn the oven down, or cover loosely with foil if it is browning too fast, although the chicken skin should be dark golden and a little charred.

**4.** Scatter with the parsley, just before serving straight from the tin, or transfer to a serving platter or dish if you prefer.

### Get Ahead

Prepare to the end of step 2 up to 3 hours ahead. The garlic, chorizo and chicken thighs can be prepared 1–2 days in advance and kept covered, individually, in the fridge.

### Hints & Tips

- If the thighs are particularly large, they will take a little longer to cook.
- Very thinly sliced chorizo, dry-fried until crisp and scattered over the top before serving, makes a lovely final flourish.
- Fresh chorizo sausages can be substituted for the chicken. They will take less time to cook.

# BAKED GREEK-STYLE STUFFED PEPPERS

SERVES 4 AS A MAIN COURSE (8 AS AN ACCOMPANIMENT OR STARTER)

4 red peppers, halved through the stalk and seeded
olive oil
1 onion, finely chopped
2 cloves of garlic, crushed
a good pinch of dried oregano
4 rashers of streaky bacon, snipped into batons
125g (4½oz) mushrooms such as shiitake, roughly chopped
a handful of pine nuts, toasted
2 tbsp sun-dried tomato purée
125g (4½oz) basmati rice
350ml (12fl oz) chicken or vegetable stock (or 1 stock cube)
2 tbsp dried breadcrumbs
salt and freshly ground black pepper

SERVING SUGGESTIONS

Rocket leaves, fresh oregano sprigs, roughly chopped parsley, black olives, tzatziki (see step 3, page 87), natural yoghurt

**I can't resist stuffed peppers when I'm in Greece! Very tasty and versatile, these are good for supper or lunch, as a starter or part of a buffet, for picnics and as an accompaniment to barbecued food. Omit the bacon and use vegetable stock, not chicken, for a lovely vegetarian main course.**

1. Cook the peppers in a large pan of well-salted, boiling water for 10 minutes. Drain well, upside down, then arrange them in a lightly oiled, shallow ovenproof dish into which they fit fairly snugly in one layer.

2. Preheat the oven to 200°C.

3. Heat a little olive oil in a saucepan and cook the onion until beginning to soften. Add the garlic, oregano and bacon, and cook for a few more minutes before adding the mushrooms and some seasoning. Cook rapidly, stirring, until any moisture has evaporated.

4. Add the pine nuts, tomato purée and rice, and stir to coat. Pour in the chicken stock, bring to the boil and adjust the seasoning if necessary. Cover with a lid and simmer very slowly for 15–20 minutes until all the liquid has absorbed and the rice is cooked – a little bite is fine, as it will swell further in the oven. Check the seasoning – it should be very well seasoned.

5. Divide the mixture between the peppers and sprinkle with dried breadcrumbs. Swirl over a good glug of olive oil, add a splash of water to the bottom of the dish and cook for 50–60 minutes or until brown and possibly a little charred. If browning too fast, cover loosely with foil. Serve lukewarm or at room temperature, *but not piping hot*, scattered with your choice of the serving suggestions (see left) and a swirl of olive oil.

**Get Ahead**

Make up to 3 days ahead, cool, cover and chill. Warm through when required or just serve at room temperature.

**Hints & Tips**

- **Buying peppers:** For stuffing, always choose female peppers, which have four rounded sections at the base and will therefore sit flat in the dish when halved, rather than tip over and spill out the contents. (A male pepper has three rounded sections and will not sit flat.)
- Almost any meat, vegetables or other leftovers can be added to the rice mixture.

# PORK, CIDER & APPLE HOTPOT

SERVES 4

**olive oil**
**4 x pork shoulder steaks, or spare rib chops (bone in or out)**
**1 onion, sliced**
**1 cooking apple, peeled and cut into postage-stamp-sized chunks**
**a sprig of sage leaves, chopped (or use a good pinch of dried)**
**½ tbsp flour**
**1 heaped tsp Dijon mustard**
**300ml (10fl oz) cider**
**150ml (5fl oz) chicken stock (or 1 stock cube)**
**500g (1lb 2oz) potatoes, peeled**
**a knob of butter**
**a little sage and/or parsley, chopped**
**salt and freshly ground black pepper**

**Get Ahead**

This can be cooked entirely up to 2 days in advance, and reheated. This will enhance the flavour.

**An easy, comforting one-pot winter warmer!**

1. Preheat the oven to 170°C.

2. Heat a little oil in a heavy-based flameproof casserole dish into which the pork steaks will fit snugly in one layer. Rub the steaks with a little salt and brown in the casserole on both sides. You will need to do this in two batches and may need to add a little more oil. Set aside on a plate.

3. Add a little more oil to the casserole dish, add the onion and cook over a medium heat until softened and just beginning to colour. Add the apple and sage and some seasoning, and cook for a few more minutes. Stir in the flour and mustard, pour in the cider and stock, and bring to the boil, stirring. Check the seasoning and adjust accordingly. Nestle the pork into the bottom of the casserole dish and set aside.

4. Cut the potatoes into 5mm- (¼in-) thick slices and arrange them, overlapping, over the top of the pork. Season with salt and pepper, and dot with a little butter. Bring to the boil and cover with the lid.

5. Transfer to the preheated oven and cook for 1 hour, then remove the lid and cook for a further hour. Turn the oven up high to crisp and brown further at the end of cooking, if necessary, bearing in mind it will only ever be pale golden and reasonably crispy. Rest for 10–15 minutes before eating, although it will happily wait for an hour or more. Scatter with sage and/or parsley before serving.

# SAUSAGE & PUY LENTIL CASSEROLE WITH ROASTED BUTTERNUT SQUASH

SERVES 4

olive oil
8 sausages
1 onion, finely chopped
2 rashers of streaky bacon, snipped into strips
1 carrot, diced
3 cloves of garlic, crushed
3 sprigs of fresh thyme, or a good pinch of dried
225g (8oz) Puy lentils
500ml (18fl oz) chicken stock (or 2 stock cubes)
salt and freshly ground black pepper
1 small butternut squash
Dijon mustard
freshly chopped parsley, to garnish (optional)

**Get Ahead**

Prepare to the end of step 4 up to 2 days ahead. Cool, cover and refrigerate individually. Reheat both components in a moderate oven when required.

**Be adventurous with the sausages you use, and buy the best you can afford. I like spicy Italian ones, which often contain fennel, as well as chilli sausages, Toulouse sausages, fresh chorizo or just good farmhouse sausages.**

**1.** Preheat the oven to 220°C.

**2.** Heat a little oil in a sauté pan that has a lid or in a shallow casserole dish. Brown the sausages all over and remove to a plate. Add the onion, bacon and carrot and a little more olive oil, if necessary, and fry until beginning to soften, then add the garlic and thyme, and cook for a further minute.

**3.** Add the lentils and stir over the heat for a minute or so, before adding the stock and plenty of black pepper (no salt at this stage). Return the sausages to the pan. Bring to the boil, cover and simmer very gently for 25 minutes or until the lentils are cooked but still have a little bite to them – they shouldn't be mushy. Season with salt.

**4.** Meanwhile, halve the butternut squash (no need to peel it), remove the seeds and cut into bite-sized chunks. Toss with a little olive oil and salt in a roasting tin or on a baking sheet, spread out in one layer, and cook at the top of the oven for 20–30 minutes or until beginning to brown and caramelize, turning once halfway through.

**5.** Serve the casserole with a little Dijon mustard blobbed over the top, followed by the butternut squash and a sprinkling of roughly chopped parsley, if using. Or, if you prefer, serve the squash separately.

# AUBERGINE PARMIGIANA



SERVES 6–8 AS AN ACCOMPANIMENT

**3–4 medium aubergines (roughly 1kg/2lb 4oz)**
**olive oil**
**2 x 125g (4½oz) mozzarella balls (in liquid), thinly sliced**
**100g (3½oz) Parmesan cheese, grated**
**a few dried breadcrumbs**
**salt and freshly ground black pepper**
**fresh basil leaves, to serve**

FOR THE TOMATO SAUCE

**a glug of olive oil**
**2 cloves of garlic, crushed**
**a large pinch of dried oregano**
**400g (14oz) tin of chopped tomatoes, rinsed out with ½ a tin of water**
**1 tbsp sun-dried tomato purée**
**½ tsp sugar**

### Get Ahead

Prepare to the end of step 4 up to 24 hours in advance. Cool, cover and refrigerate. Bring back to room temperature at least 1 hour before cooking. Don't be alarmed at the liquid that will have seeped out – all will be well.

**This classic Italian dish is delicious as a main course in its own right, as an accompaniment or as an antipasto. Just as welcome in the colder months as it is in the summer, it pairs beautifully with meat, poultry and fish, and is lovely with barbecued food.**

**1.** Preheat the oven to 220°C.

**2.** Slice the aubergines in half lengthways, then each half into three slices about 1cm (½in) thick, and arrange them on a large, lightly oiled baking sheet in one layer. You will need to do this in two batches (or use two baking sheets). Scatter with salt and drizzle with a little olive oil. Bake at the very top of the oven for 10–15 minutes or until deep golden brown on the underside. Turn them over and repeat on the other side, although this will take less time. Set aside. Turn the oven down to 200°C.

**3.** Meanwhile, for the sauce, heat a little olive oil in a saucepan, add the garlic and oregano, and cook for a minute or so, then add the rest of the tomato sauce ingredients. Bring to the boil and simmer gently for 5–10 minutes.

**4.** Grease a shallow ovenproof dish (approximately 28 x 23cm/11 x 9in) with olive oil and spread a thin layer (roughly one-third) of the tomato sauce over the bottom. Cover with half the aubergine slices, followed by half the mozzarella, breaking it up as you go for even distribution, then a good scattering of Parmesan and some seasoning. Repeat this layering, finishing with the final third of the tomato sauce roughly spread over the top.

**5.** Scatter with the remaining Parmesan, a few dried breadcrumbs and a good dribble of olive oil. Bake for 35–40 minutes or until golden brown and bubbling. Leave to cool until lukewarm and scatter with a few torn basil leaves before serving.

### Hints & Tips

- This is best eaten lukewarm – not piping hot. It's very good when reheated, too.
- Serve with a green salad and some new potatoes to eke it out as a main course.
- A layer of cooked lamb or chicken in the middle is a lovely addition.
- It will keep for 5 days or so in the fridge once cooked.

# SRI LANKAN BEETROOT CURRY

SERVES 6 AS AN ACCOMPANIMENT

vegetable oil
1 large onion, sliced
4–5 medium raw beetroot, peeled
2 cloves of garlic, crushed
1 tsp curry powder
½ tsp garam masala
a small handful of dried curry leaves, roughly crushed in your palm
⅛ tsp chilli powder
1 tsp salt
freshly ground black pepper
400g (14oz) tin of coconut milk
natural yoghurt, roughly chopped parsley, yellow mustard seeds (optional)

SERVING SUGGESTIONS

Rice, Sri Lankan Prawn Curry (see page 102), Dhal (see page 103), flatbreads, poppadums

**Get Ahead**

Make to the end of step 4 up to 2 days in advance, cool, cover and refrigerate.

**Despite being called a curry, this doesn't have to be spicy hot, thus making it a lovely vegetable accompaniment not only to other curries, but also to plain roast meats, poultry and game, as well as fish and steak. Delicious, too, in its own right and ideal for vegetarians.**

1. Heat a little oil in a sauté pan or wok, add the onion and cook slowly until soft.

2. Meanwhile, process the beetroot into thin chips, or fat matchsticks, using the chip or julienne strip attachment of a food processor. Alternatively, cut into chunky matchsticks by hand.

3. When the onions are cooked, add all the remaining ingredients, except the beetroot and coconut milk, and cook, stirring, for a few minutes until the spices become fragrant.

4. If the pan is dry, heat a little more oil, then add the beetroot. Cook slowly for 5–10 minutes, stirring occasionally, or until softened but still with some bite. (The time will depend on the thickness and age of the beetroot.) Add half the tin of coconut milk, bring to the boil, cover with a lid and simmer gently for a few minutes – the beetroot must still retain some bite. Set aside until required.

5. Just before serving, gradually add the rest of the coconut milk (you might not need it all) swirling it in, to give a purple and white ripple effect. If using, dribble with yoghurt and scatter with parsley and mustard seeds.

# SRI LANKAN PRAWN CURRY

SERVES 6

vegetable oil
1 onion, finely sliced
3 cloves of garlic, crushed
a small handful of dried curry leaves, roughly crushed in your palm
⅛ tsp chilli powder (or ¼ tsp, if you like)
2 tsp garam masala
1 tsp curry powder
1 tsp salt
¼ tsp turmeric
¼ tsp coarsely ground black pepper
a pinch of ground cinnamon
1 tsp ginger, grated (or ready-prepared from a jar)
1½ x 400g (14oz) tins of coconut milk, possibly a little more
900g (2lb) raw, shelled prawns (frozen weight), thawed and well drained
natural yoghurt, to serve
a few sprigs of coriander or parsley (optional)

SERVING SUGGESTIONS

Rice, Sri Lankan Beetroot Curry (see page 100), Dhal (see opposite), flatbreads, poppadums, green vegetables

**I learnt to make this delicious curry, and many others too, from a Sinhalese cook while I was in Sri Lanka. I have reduced the heat somewhat, but it can be ramped up as much as you like by adding more chilli powder. It's unbelievably quick to make and perfect for get-ahead entertaining.**

**1.** Heat a little vegetable oil in a sauté pan or wok, and cook the onions until soft. Add the rest of the ingredients, except the coconut milk and prawns, and cook for a further few minutes until the spices become fragrant.

**2.** Stir in the coconut milk, bring to the boil and simmer gently for 7–10 minutes. Check and adjust the seasoning accordingly.

**3.** Just before serving, bring the sauce back to the boil and add the drained prawns, a handful at a time. You may need to add some more coconut milk. Cook, stirring, for a few minutes until the prawns have barely turned pink – this will take no time at all, and they will become rubbery and inedible if cooked any longer. Serve topped with blobs of yoghurt and scatter with herbs, if using.

### Get Ahead

Prepare to the end of step 2 up to 3 days in advance. Continue with step 3 just before serving. The prawns can be thawed and drained 24 hours ahead and kept covered in the fridge.

### Hints & Tips

- This is a generous amount of prawns for 6 people, so depending on what else you are serving, it would easily stretch to 7 or 8 people.
- It's far cheaper to buy frozen prawns and thaw them, than to buy them ready-thawed.
- If there is any leftover coconut milk, it can be frozen.

# DHAL

SERVES 6

160g (5½oz) red split lentils
3 cloves of garlic, crushed
a small handful of dried curry leaves, roughly crushed
1 tsp salt
1½ tsp curry powder
a good pinch of ground cinnamon
½ tsp turmeric
⅛ tsp chilli powder, or a whole chilli, halved
2 tomatoes, roughly chopped
1 small onion, sliced

FOR THE TARKA

vegetable oil
1 shallot, sliced
1 tsp black mustard seeds
1 tsp cumin seeds
a few dried chilli flakes
a few curry leaves, crushed

SERVING SUGGESTIONS

Natural yoghurt, roughly chopped coriander or parsley leaves, plus see Hints & Tips (far right)

**I could quite happily eat dhal every day in winter – a very healthy, vegetarian 'hug in a bowl' and the essence of comfort food. Enjoy it in its simplest form, or add any number of other goodies to it – see below for some ideas. Very good, too, with the Sri Lankan curries on page 100 and opposite.**

**1.** Put all the dhal ingredients into a saucepan with 700ml (1¼ pints) water. Bring to the boil and simmer, uncovered, for 35 minutes, giving it a stir every so often, until soft or the required consistency. However, bear in mind it will thicken up as it cools and stands, if not using straightaway. Check and adjust the seasoning if necessary.

**2.** For the tarka, heat a good glug of vegetable oil in a small pan and fry the shallot for a few minutes until brown and crispy. Add the rest of the ingredients and cook for a further minute or so. Set aside if not using straightaway (reheat before serving).

**3.** Reheat the dhal, if necessary, and put into a serving dish or bowl. Just before serving, pile the hot sizzling tarka into the middle of the dhal. Finally, adorn with yoghurt and herbs, if using.

**Get Ahead**

Make to the end of step 2 up to 3 days in advance. You may or may not need to thin the dhal with a little water.

**Hints & Tips**

**A few embellishments to stir in at the end:** Raw spinach, grated courgette, finely shredded kale, chard, spring greens or sprouts; cooked diced carrot, aubergine or okra; tinned chickpeas. And you can never go wrong with a soft-boiled, poached or fried egg on top!

# FEASTS FOR · FRIENDS ·

# STUFFED PORK FILLET WITH WILD MUSHROOM SAUCE

SERVES 4–6 (DEPENDING ON SIZE OF FILLET)

**olive oil**
**1 shallot, finely chopped**
**1 clove of garlic, crushed**
**140g (5oz) mushrooms, such as shiitake, chestnut or mixed, chopped**
**30g (1oz) walnut pieces (a handful), roughly chopped**
**a handful of parsley, chopped**
**1 fillet of pork, trimmed of its silvery membrane**
**5 slices of Parma ham**
**salt and freshly ground black pepper**
**pork skin, for crackling (optional, see Pork Scratchings, page 20)**
**watercress, for decorating (optional)**

FOR THE WILD MUSHROOM SAUCE

**8–10g (¼oz) dried wild mushrooms (mixed are fine)**
**85g (3oz) fresh mushrooms, chopped**
**olive oil**
**300ml (10fl oz) chicken stock**
**3 heaped tbsp crème fraîche (or 4–5 tbsp double cream)**
**a handful of parsley, chopped**

TO SERVE

**Orzo or trofie pasta, rice, mashed or new potatoes, a green vegetable**

### Get Ahead

Make to the end of step 4 up to a day ahead. The sauce (step 5) can be made up to 3 days ahead or freeze, but add the parsley just before serving.

**This is one of my most popular recipes for entertaining and can be completely prepared ahead. It's an inexpensive way of feeding a lot of people, too.**

1. Heat a little olive oil in a frying pan and cook the shallot, garlic and mushrooms with some seasoning until soft, beginning to brown and the mixture is dry. Add the walnuts and the parsley, check the seasoning and spread out on a plate to cool.

2. Preheat the oven to 220°C. Lightly oil a roasting tin into which the pork fits snugly.

3. Cut the pork fillet along its length, to about a quarter of its thickness, leaving 1cm (½in) at each end uncut. Open out as flat as you can by cutting long incisions inside the pocket but not cutting right through. Or, having made the first cut, bat it out flat between two sheets of clingfilm. Spread the stuffing along the fillet.

4. Lay the Parma ham slices out vertically, slightly overlapping, on a piece of clingfilm or baking paper. They should be roughly the same length as the fillet. Re-form the fillet, enclosing the stuffing as best you can and place it, cut-side down, along the middle of the Parma ham sheet. Fold the Parma ham up over the pork from each side to enclose it. Transfer to the roasting tin, seam-side down.

5. For the sauce, break the dried mushrooms into small pieces and cover with hot water in a small bowl. Soak for 30 minutes, strain, remove any grit and reserve the liquid. Cook the fresh mushrooms in a little oil until soft and the moisture has evaporated. Add the soaked mushrooms and cook for another minute, then add the stock and reserved mushroom liquid. Bring to the boil, then simmer for 10–15 minutes until reduced a little. Stir in the crème fraîche (or double cream) and bubble up. Add the parsley just before serving.

6. Drizzle the pork with olive oil and cook for 15 minutes until brown and crispy. Remove from the tin and rest it somewhere warm for 20 minutes or up to an hour.

7. Cut diagonally into 1cm- (½in-) thick slices and serve on a platter with the watercress, if using. Pour any juices from the pork into the sauce. Spoon a little sauce over the pork, top with the crackling, if using, and serve the remaining sauce separately. Surround the pork with orzo pasta on one side and green vegetables on the other to create an eye-catching feast.

### Hints & Tips

- Use the Parma ham straight from the fridge or it'll be impossible to manipulate. Buy a few extra slices in case you need to stem any leaks.
- Fillets vary from 340–560g (12oz–1lb 4oz), giving 16–22 slices; the cooking time will be the same.
- Try the sauce with steak and chicken.

# CHICKEN LEGS BAKED WITH OLIVES & CAPERS

SERVES 4

4 chicken legs, trimmed
5 cloves of garlic, crushed
a few sprigs of fresh oregano or ½ tsp dried
3 tbsp red wine vinegar
3 tbsp olive oil
¾ tsp salt
freshly ground black pepper
100g (3½oz) green olives, pitted
60g (2oz) capers, plus 2 tbsp of their liquid
70g (2½oz) dates or prunes, pitted and quartered lengthways
2 bay leaves
125ml (4fl oz) white wine
1 tbsp dark muscovado or soft dark brown sugar
freshly chopped parsley or sprigs of fresh oregano, to garnish

SERVING SUGGESTIONS

Mashed or new potatoes; a green vegetable

**This is my variation of the classic recipe from the iconic *The Silver Palate Cookbook* by Julee Rosso and Sheila Lukins with Michael McLaughlin, published in New York in 1982. Very easy to make and ideal for a quick supper, it also lends itself beautifully to entertaining, as everything can be prepared days in advance, leaving nothing to do at the last minute. An extremely popular and useful recipe – quite simply, it is delicious!**

1. Put the chicken legs into a non-reactive bowl or dish, skin-side up.

2. Add all the ingredients except for the wine, brown sugar and garnish, and mix everything together. Cover and leave to marinate at room temperature for an hour or so, and then put into the fridge for up to 2 days, turning and basting occasionally – just whenever you remember.

3. Preheat the oven to 220°C.

4. Put the chicken legs, with the marinade, into a shallow ovenproof serving dish or roasting tin into which they fit snugly in one layer. Pour the wine around and sprinkle the sugar over the top of the legs. Roast at the top of the oven on the highest shelf for 50–60 minutes, until golden brown and the chicken is cooked through. You may need to loosely drape a piece of foil over the top if it's browning too quickly or lower the oven shelf. Bear in mind that the chicken skin should be charred – almost blackened, in fact.

5. Scatter with chopped parsley or sprigs of fresh oregano and serve.

**Get Ahead**

Prepare to the end of step 2 up to 2 days ahead. Marinating for 24 or even 48 hours is good, but don't worry if you haven't time – it'll still be delicious!

**Hints & Tips**

Substitute the legs with chicken thighs, allowing two per person.

# DUCK CONFIT & CELERIAC PURÉE WITH CHERRY SAUCE

SERVES 4

4 tsp sea salt
6 juniper berries, coarsely crushed
2 cloves of garlic, sliced
8 black peppercorns, coarsely crushed, (or a pinch of ground black pepper)
2 sprigs of fresh thyme or 1 tsp dried
4 duck legs, trimmed
2 bay leaves

FOR THE CHERRY SAUCE
4 tbsp good-quality cherry jam
2 tbsp soy sauce
2 tbsp red wine vinegar
1 tsp fresh ginger, chopped (or ready-prepared from a jar)
1 tsp fish sauce

FOR THE CELERIAC PURÉE
1 large bulb of celeriac (approximately 1.2kg/2½lb)
freshly squeezed juice of ½ a lemon
salt and freshly ground black pepper
a generous knob of butter
whole nutmeg, for grating
cream (optional)

### Get Ahead

- Prepare to the end of step 2 up to 2 days ahead, cover and refrigerate. Bring back to room temperature an hour or so before cooking.
- The sauce (step 3) can be made up to 4 days in advance, as can the Celeriac Purée (steps 5–6), which reheats very quickly in a saucepan, medium oven or microwave. It also freezes very well.

**A very tasty and easy get-ahead recipe that is perfect for entertaining, as there is nothing to do at the last minute. Braised Leeks with Herbs & Peas (see page 144) is a lovely accompaniment. You will need to start this recipe a day ahead.**

1. Mix together all the duck ingredients, except for the duck legs and bay leaves. Put the legs, skin-side down, into a shallow non-reactive dish and rub half the mixture into the flesh. Turn them over and repeat on the skin side, then nestle in the bay leaves. Cover, leave at room temperature for an hour, then refrigerate for 24 hours.

2. After 24 hours, wash all the salt mixture off the legs under cold running water. Dry them on kitchen paper.

3. Mix all the sauce ingredients together in a small saucepan with 1 tablespoon of water and slowly bring to the boil, stirring to help dissolve the jam. Taste and adjust accordingly: you may like to make it more sweet, sour or savoury, bearing in mind it will taste much sweeter and stronger in this concentrated form than when served in a small quantity with the duck.

4. Preheat the oven to 180°C. Put the legs, skin-side up, into a lightly greased shallow roasting tin or ovenproof dish and cook in the preheated oven for 1¼ hours until golden and crispy.

5. Meanwhile, peel the celeriac and cut into even-sized chunks. Place in a saucepan of salted water with the lemon juice and its squeezed shell. Bring to the boil, then simmer for 20–30 minutes until tender.

6. Drain, discarding the lemon shell, and leave for a few minutes in the colander to steam dry. Process, or mash, with a generous knob of butter, grating of nutmeg and seasoning, until smooth. Check the seasoning and process again with a splash of cream, if using.

7. Reheat the sauce and the Celeriac Purée. Heap the celeriac onto a platter, prop the duck legs up against it with the drumsticks sticking up and dribble a little sauce over the legs. Serve the rest separately – it's not gravy and a little goes a long way.

### Hints & Tips

- I often serve the duck legs without the sauce. They are also delicious with Celeriac Rémoulade (see page 155) and/or braised Puy lentils.
- The cooked duck, plus crispy skin, can be removed from the bones, shredded and rolled up in Chinese pancakes, or made into spring rolls using spring roll wrappers.
- The cherry sauce is very good with duck breasts, cooked as usual and served pink and sliced, with noodles.

# STICKY ROAST QUAIL WITH HERBY LEMON MAFTOUL



SERVES 4

4 tsp ras el hanout (a North African spice mix)
1 tsp ground cumin
3 tbsp olive oil
1 tbsp pomegranate molasses
8 oven-ready quail, untrussed
salt

FOR THE HERBY MAFTOUL
255g (9oz) maftoul (giant couscous)
salt
olive oil
1 bunch of spring onions, trimmed and thinly sliced diagonally
a handful of mint, chopped
a handful of parsley, chopped
a handful of coriander, chopped
a good handful of pine nuts, toasted
1–2 tbsp pomegranate seeds

FOR THE LEMON DRESSING
zest and freshly squeezed juice of 1 lemon
3 tbsp olive oil
salt

TO SERVE
Natural yoghurt, mixed with seasoning, a little olive oil and thinned with water if necessary (optional)

**Warm and spicy, very tasty, and perfect for relaxed sharing. Serve lukewarm or at room temperature, piled onto a platter and let everyone dig in. Maftoul, or giant couscous, looks like small pearls and, unlike couscous, has a nice chewy bite to it.**

1. Mix the spices, olive oil and molasses into a paste in a bowl. Add the quail and coat all over with the paste. Leave to marinate for an hour, or longer if possible.

2. Preheat the oven to 220°C. Arrange the quail in a lightly greased shallow roasting tin into which they fit quite snugly, but without touching. Sprinkle generously with salt and a little olive oil, and roast for 20 minutes until golden, crispy and possibly a little charred.

3. Meanwhile, add the maftoul to a large pan of well-salted boiling water and cook until tender, about 6–8 minutes, but be guided by the packet instructions. Drain well and if not serving hot, or immediately, run briefly under cold water to stop it cooking. Either way, put it into a bowl and stir in a tiny bit of oil to stop it from sticking.

4. Mix the lemon dressing ingredients together.

5. Just before serving, mix the maftoul with the rest of its ingredients, except for the pomegranate seeds, followed by the dressing. Pile up in the middle of a large platter, arrange the quail over the top and scatter with the pomegranate seeds. Serve with a jug of the roasting juices, scraped from the tin and bubbled up with a little water, and the yoghurt sauce, if using.

**Get Ahead**

- Prepare the quail to step 1 up to a day ahead.
- Cook the maftoul (step 3) and prepare the lemon dressing (step 4) up to 2 days in advance and keep them separately in the fridge, covered. Bring the maftoul back to room temperature or warm through in a saucepan with a little oil before serving. The spring onions can be sliced 24 hours ahead. The herbs can be chopped any time on the day and added just before serving.

**Hints & Tips**

- One quail each might suffice for some, but remember they are very small.
- Substitute one small poussin per person for the quail. Roast for 35–40 minutes at the same temperature, and cover loosely with foil if getting too brown towards the end of the cooking time.
- Maftoul is delicious served with meat, poultry, fish and stews. You can also use it as the base for numerous salads. Try adding feta cheese, red onion, rocket, preserved lemons, sun-dried tomatoes, chopped fresh tomatoes, cucumber, chickpeas, lentils, saffron, dates, figs and so on.

# TAGLIATA

SERVES 4

**3 x 225g (8oz) sirloin steaks (hung for at least 3 weeks, if possible)**
**olive oil**
**salt**
**100g (3½oz) rocket**
**100g (3½oz) watercress**
**good-quality extra virgin olive oil**
**sea salt**
**a few small capers, for scattering**
**good-quality balsamic vinegar**
**Parmesan or Pecorino cheese, for shaving**
**caperberries (optional)**
**baby cherry tomatoes on the vine, roasted (see Hints & Tips, below right, optional)**

**This is one of those recipes that tastes far better than the sum of its parts. An elegant way of feeding a gathering, and eking out steak, it's simple, straightforward and healthy – and looks good, too. I usually serve this with the irresistible Roasted Crushed New Potatoes with Rosemary (see page 142).**

1. Heat a griddle, frying pan or barbecue until very hot.

2. Smear the steaks with a little olive oil and pouring salt. Cook for 1½–2 minutes on each side for rare steak, depending on their thickness. Transfer to a plate and leave to rest somewhere warm for 10 minutes. Depending on the size of the griddle or frying pan, the steaks will almost certainly need to be cooked in batches.

3. Meanwhile, scatter the rocket and watercress over a large platter and drizzle with a little extra virgin olive oil. Thinly slice the steaks diagonally and arrange artistically on top of the leaves, leaving a margin of green showing around the edges.

4. Scatter over some sea salt and a few capers, then dribble over a little balsamic vinegar and some extra virgin olive oil. Using a vegetable peeler, shave some Parmesan or Pecorino cheese over the top. Garnish with caperberries and roast baby cherry tomatoes, if using.

### Get Ahead

- Remove the steaks from the fridge an hour or so before cooking.
- If serving the steaks at room temperature, they can be cooked two days in advance and sliced when required.
- The tomatoes, if using, can be cooked (see right) up to 2 days ahead and reheated when required, or served at room temperature.

### Hints & Tips

To roast the baby cherry tomatoes on the vine, snip long vines into smaller sections or bunches, place them on a foil-lined baking sheet, drizzle with a little olive oil and sprinkle with sea salt. Roast in a hot oven for 5–10 minutes, until just softened and the skins are beginning to burst. The tomatoes should still be intact.

# SLOW-BRAISED PORK BELLY WITH SWEET CHILLI SAUCE

SERVES 8

**1 tbsp fennel seeds**
**1 tsp sea salt, plus a little extra**
**1.8kg (4lb) belly pork, individually boned, skin on and scored (boned weight)**
**225ml (8fl oz) cider or apple juice**
**vegetable oil**
**500g (1lb 2oz) fresh, cooked egg noodles**
**sesame oil (optional)**
**spring onions and red chilli, sliced into very thin long strips (optional)**

FOR THE SWEET CHILLI SAUCE

**4 tbsp soy sauce**
**4 tbsp oyster sauce**
**4 tbsp sweet chilli sauce**
**2 tsp fresh ginger, grated (or ready-prepared from a jar)**
**2 cloves of garlic, crushed**

### Get Ahead

Make to the end of step 4 up to 3 days in advance and keep it covered in the fridge.

**A winner for entertaining! Pak choi, shredded Savoy cabbage (see page 151), spinach or Swiss chard are excellent accompaniments. This needs to be started the day before.**

1. Preheat the oven to 170°C.

2. Using a herb grinder or pestle and mortar, grind the fennel seeds and 1 tsp of sea salt together. Rub this mixture all over the pork, massaging it into the nooks and crannies, and put into a lidded sauté pan or casserole, skin-side up. Pour in the cider or apple juice, bring to the boil, then cover with a piece of greaseproof or baking paper, tucking it down inside, and the lid. Transfer to the preheated oven and cook for 2 hours.

3. Leave in the pan until just warm, then remove the pork from the liquid and press between two trays with weights on top, cover and refrigerate overnight.

4. Mix all the sauce ingredients together and set aside.

5. To serve, preheat the oven to 220°C. Line a roasting tin with foil.

6. Trim off the edges of the pork, rub the skin with a little vegetable oil and salt, cut into 16 squares and place on a greased rack over the foil-lined tin. Cook for 15–20 minutes until hot and golden brown. The skin may or may not crackle; either way, it will still be tender, gelatinous and tasty.

7. Meanwhile, heat the noodles by tossing them in a pan with a little hot sesame oil or covering them with boiling water for a few minutes. Drain. Serve, topped with the pork and the spring onions and red chilli, if using, and a little of the sauce spooned over the top. Serve the rest of the sauce separately.

### Hints & Tips

- Cut the pork into chunky slices instead of squares, if you prefer.
- The sauce is strong so a little goes a long way – it's not gravy!
- This makes a delicious warm starter or lunch, sliced and cooked until golden, crisp and sizzling, sitting atop some salad leaves, with a few shallots and gherkins and some punchy seedy mustard dressing.
- If using dried noodles, you will need a smaller quantity.
- If you don't have a large enough pan or casserole dish with a lid, use a snug-fitting roasting tin and cover with foil as well as the paper.
- Scrunched-up foil works just as well as a rack when reheating the pork. If it's reheated sitting directly on the bottom of a tin, it will burn.

# TURKEY, MUSHROOM & TARRAGON PITHIVIERS

SERVES 6–8

**55g (2oz) butter**
**1 onion, finely chopped**
**1 stick of celery, chopped**
**1 tbsp freshly chopped tarragon or ½ tbsp dried**
**110g (4oz) chestnut mushrooms, sliced**
**450g (1lb) turkey meat, cut roughly into 1cm (½in) chunks, raw or cooked**
**2 tbsp plain flour**
**1 tbsp Dijon mustard**
**4 tbsp dry sherry**
**freshly squeezed juice of ½ a lemon (1 tbsp)**
**150ml (5fl oz) chicken stock (or ½ a stock cube)**
**4 tbsp crème fraîche (or double cream)**
**a handful of fresh parsley, leaves chopped**
**500g (1lb 2oz) block of puff pastry**
**1 egg, beaten with a little salt, to glaze**
**poppy or nigella seeds (optional)**
**sea salt and freshly ground black pepper**

### Get Ahead

Make to the end of step 6 up to 2 days ahead, cover and refrigerate.

**What could be nicer than a luscious creamy filling encased in puff pastry? This is a savoury take on the classic French almond pie and a very tasty way of using up leftovers, although, more often than not, I make it with fresh turkey or chicken. Ideally, the filling should be made the day before. Considerably easier than it looks!**

1. Melt the butter in a deep-sided sauté pan. Add the onion and celery, cook gently until softened, then add the tarragon and mushrooms, and cook until just beginning to brown around the edges.

2. If using raw turkey, add to the pan and fry until it has turned opaque, then add the flour, mustard, sherry, lemon juice and stock. If using cooked turkey, add at the same time as the flour.

3. Bring to the boil (the mixture will be very thick) and simmer for a few minutes. Stir in the crème fraîche, check the seasoning, tip into a bowl and leave to cool, preferably overnight in the fridge, as it needs to be cold and thick. Stir in the parsley.

4. Preheat the oven to 200°C. Put in a flat baking sheet to warm.

5. Cut the puff pastry in half and roll both halves into two rough circles. Using a plate as a template (about 27cm/10¾in), cut out two circles, one slightly larger than the other. Put the smaller circle onto a piece of silicone paper. Lightly score a rim 2cm (¾in) around the edge.

6. Spoon the cold turkey mixture into the middle of the smaller pastry circle, giving it some height in the middle and leaving the rim bare. Brush the rim with egg glaze, being careful not to get glaze on the cut edges. Lay the larger pastry circle over the top, press the edges together and push them up using a sharp knife or crimp. Very carefully score the top with semi-circular lines running from the middle down to the edge at 1cm (½in) intervals.

7. Brush with egg glaze, sprinkle with a little sea salt and a few poppy or nigella seeds, if using. Carefully slide the pithivier onto the hot baking sheet and bake for 20 minutes or until puffed up and golden brown.

### Hints & Tips

- Substitute pheasant, chicken, rabbit, ham, bacon or vegetables and cheese for the turkey.
- The filling is delicious on its own with rice – just make the sauce runnier.
- Turkey gravy can be used instead of the sauce, as long as it's thick when cold – just add crème fraîche.
- Don't worry if the pastry bursts open a little – it will still taste delicious.

# SPATCHCOCK HARISSA CHICKEN WITH YOGHURT & MINT SAUCE

SERVES 4–6

**1.6–1.8kg (3½–4lb) chicken**
**salt**

FOR THE MARINADE
**150g (5½oz) natural yoghurt**
**1 tbsp rose harissa**
**1 tbsp vegetable oil**
**2 cloves of garlic, crushed**

FOR THE YOGHURT & MINT SAUCE
**200g (7oz) natural yoghurt**
**a handful of chopped mint**
**salt and freshly ground black pepper**

SERVING SUGGESTION
**naan bread**

**Get Ahead**
Prepare to the end of step 3 up to 24 hours in advance.

**Hints & Tips**
- Very good cooked on a barbecue.
- Alternatively, spatchcock individual poussins in the same way, which also saves carving or jointing. Chicken thighs and legs are other substitutes – slash them before marinating.
- A 2kg (4½lb) chicken feeds 6 easily.

**When spatchcocked, birds cook much more quickly, are easier to carve and have crispier skin than when roasted whole. During marination, the acid in yoghurt activates enzymes in poultry and meat, which break down the proteins, making it super tender and super juicy. Fattoush (see page 154) and/or Kisir (see page 149) are perfect accompaniments.**

1. Mix all the marinade ingredients together.

2. Turn the chicken onto its breast and, with a pair of scissors, snip down both sides of the backbone (starting on either side of the parson's nose) and discard. Pull out any lumps of fat, turn over and press down hard with the heel of your hand to flatten the chicken. Cut out the wishbone for easier carving, if you like. Using a knife, slash the flesh through its fattest parts – twice through the breasts and twice through the legs.

3. Put the chicken into a bowl and smear all over with the marinade. Leave to marinate, flesh-side down, in the fridge for up to 24 hours (although even an hour or two is fine and better than nothing at all).

4. Preheat the oven to 200°C. Use baking parchment to line a shallow roasting tin into which the chicken will fit fairly snugly.

5. Lay the chicken out on top, skin-side up, sprinkle with a little salt and cook for 40–45 minutes (50–60 minutes for a larger chicken) or until cooked through. Check towards the end of the cooking time that it's not browning too fast; cover very loosely with foil if it is. It should be golden and a little bit charred in places. Conversely, raise the heat towards the end if it needs more browning.

6. Meanwhile, mix the sauce ingredients together and put in a small serving bowl. Serve the chicken straight from the paper-lined tin, with the pan juices poured into a little jug, some warm naan bread and the yoghurt and mint sauce.

# MONKFISH WITH PEAS, FENNEL & ROMESCO SAUCE

SERVES 4–5

1 x 450g (1lb) monkfish tail, boned into 2 fillets, or the same weight of smaller fillets
6–8 fresh sage leaves
12 rashers of pancetta or smoked streaky bacon (straight from the fridge)
450g (1lb) celeriac, peeled and cut into 1cm (½in) dice
olive oil
1 large shallot, sliced
450g (1lb) frozen petits pois
2 bulbs of fennel
½ tbsp freshly chopped mint and/or sage leaves
½ a lemon
salt and freshly ground black pepper

FOR THE ROMESCO SAUCE

3 small, or 2 large, roasted peppers from a jar, roughly chopped
1 clove of garlic, roughly chopped
½ red chilli, seeded and roughly chopped
40g (1½oz) blanched hazelnuts, toasted
1 ripe tomato, roughly chopped
1 tbsp sherry or red wine vinegar
4 tbsp olive oil

TO SERVE

Lemon wedges, fried sage leaves (optional): Fry the sage leaves briefly in a little olive oil until crisp but not browned (they crisp up more when cool), drain on kitchen paper and sprinkle with salt

**A lovely all-in-one recipe served elegantly on a platter for entertaining, or straight from the pan for supper. It's completely prepare-ahead and very easy, I promise!**

1. Preheat the oven to 220°C. Trim off any pinkish grey membrane from the monkfish. Place sage leaves along the length of one fillet, then cover with the other, top to tail.

2. Stretch out the pancetta (or bacon) using the back of a heavy knife. Lay out horizontally and slightly overlapping on a work surface, forming a 'sheet' of pancetta the same length as the fillets. Place the fillets vertically down the middle. Fold the pancetta over from each side, encasing the fish quite tightly. Set aside.

3. Process all the sauce ingredients into a textured sauce. Add more oil if you prefer it runnier. (This sauce is delicious with so many things!)

4. Cook the celeriac in a pan of boiling salted water for a few minutes until just tender. Drain and set aside. Heat a little olive oil in a large sauté pan, cook the shallot until soft, then add the peas, 1 tbsp of water and some seasoning. Cook for a few minutes until just thawed. Check the seasoning and add the celeriac. Set aside.

5. Cut off and discard the tough outer layer and tops of the fennel bulbs, reserving the ferny fronds. Halve through the root, then cut each half into three or four thin slices. Lightly oil a large baking sheet, spread the fennel out in one layer, dribble with a little olive oil and some salt, and cook at the top of the oven for 10–15 minutes until golden and caramelized, turning over halfway through. Set aside.

6. Heat a little oil in a frying pan, preferably ovenproof, and seal the wrapped fish quickly until golden on all sides, then transfer to the oven and cook for 10 minutes (transfer to a baking sheet in the absence of an ovenproof frying pan). Remove the fish to a plate and leave to rest somewhere warm for at least 10 minutes.

7. Just before serving, reheat the peas, adding the chopped herbs. Cut the monkfish into 12 diagonal slices, and arrange on top of the peas, in the pan or on a platter, with any juices poured over. Nestle the fennel in between, squeeze over the lemon and scatter with the reserved fennel fronds and fried sage leaves (see below left), if using. Serve with the Romesco sauce.

### Get Ahead

Prepare steps 1–5 up to 24 hours in advance, cover individually and refrigerate. Reheat the peas on the hob, and the fennel in the oven for 5 minutes before serving.

### Hints & Tips

- If using four smaller fillets, simply form into two parcels.
- Any leafy or (diced) root vegetables could be added to the peas, such as spinach, kale, chard or potato.

# BANG BANG CHICKEN



SERVES 6–8

**2½ tbsp granulated sugar**
**1 tsp salt**
**4 tbsp rice vinegar**
**2 medium carrots, peeled and cut into fine matchsticks**
**½ a cucumber, cut into fine matchsticks**
**a bunch of spring onions, trimmed, halved and cut into thin strips**
**1 poached (see below right) or cooked chicken, 900g–2kg (2lb–4½lb)**
**2 cos or little gem lettuces, and/or a bag of watercress**

FOR THE SAUCE

**140g (5oz) smooth peanut butter**
**1 tbsp sweet chilli sauce**
**2½ tbsp toasted sesame oil**
**3 tbsp vegetable oil**
**½ tbsp soy sauce**

SERVING SUGGESTIONS

**Roughly chopped salted peanuts, torn mint leaves, red chilli (seeded and thinly sliced diagonally), toasted black and white sesame seeds**

### Get Ahead

- The vegetables can be pickled 2 or more hours in advance, even the day before. The longer they are pickled, the softer the texture will be, but they will still retain some crunch.
- Step 2 can be prepared up to 4 days ahead. If made in advance, warm the sauce a little before using, as it will be easier to coat the chicken.
- Step 3 can be completed 2 days in advance.

**This Chinese classic is so easy to make and a real crowd-pleaser. It's very child-friendly, too – show me a child who doesn't like peanut butter and chicken! I have suggested quick-pickling the vegetables, which is delicious, and a foil to the sauce, but do skip that if you like.**

1. Heat the sugar, salt and vinegar together in a small saucepan, stir to dissolve the sugar, then simmer for 1–2 minutes until syrupy. Put the carrots, cucumber and spring onions into a small bowl, pour over the hot syrup and set aside, giving it a good stir from time to time to coat all the vegetables.

2. Place all the sauce ingredients in a small bowl and sit it over a pan of simmering water for a few minutes, whisking occasionally, until a smooth sauce has formed. The gentle heat makes it easier to meld the ingredients together (and to coat the chicken later, see step 5).

3. Meanwhile, remove the skin and bones from the chicken, discard, and tear the flesh into strips.

4. Slice the lettuce across into ribbons and scatter over a large platter (and/or the watercress, if using). Using a slotted spoon, take the vegetables out of the vinegar mixture, draining well, and arrange on top of the lettuce, leaving a rim of leaves showing around the edge.

5. Heap half the chicken on top, spoon over a little of the warm sauce (you may need to thin it with a little warm water to achieve a coating consistency), followed by the rest of the chicken and the sauce. Sprinkle with the peanuts, mint leaves, chilli and sesame seeds, if using.

## TO POACH A CHICKEN

Place the chicken in a saucepan into which it fits fairly snugly. Barely cover with water, add a quartered onion, 2 bay leaves, a few peppercorns and any other aromatics you like. Put on the lid, bring to the boil and simmer gently for 1 hour. Remove the pan from the heat and leave the chicken to cool in its liquid, although it doesn't have to be completely cold before removing.

### Hints & Tips

- Shredded mangetout and radish batons could be added to the pickle.
- Don't add water to the neat peanut butter as it will seize, but it's fine to add some to the sauce.
- This is very good made with pheasant and leftover turkey.
- Serve with chopsticks for authenticity.

# TARTE FINE WITH FILLET OF BEEF, ONION MARMALADE, PECORINO & ROCKET

MAKES 8 LARGE SQUARES (OR MANY MORE SMALLER ONES!)

**1 sheet of ready-rolled puff pastry (preferably all-butter)**
**450g (1lb) beef fillet tails, trimmed**
**olive oil**
**salt**
**½ a 325g (11½oz) jar of caramelized red onion chutney**
**2 good handfuls of rocket leaves (or watercress or salad cress)**
**sea salt and ground black pepper**
**Pecorino Romano cheese shavings (or Parmesan or Manchego)**
**a few capers**

FOR THE WATERCRESS MAYONNAISE

**3 heaped tbsp thick mayonnaise**
**3 good handfuls of watercress, tough stalks removed**
**lime juice, to taste**
**salt and freshly ground black pepper**

### Get Ahead

- Cook step 1 up to 3 days in advance, wrap in clingfilm and keep somewhere cool. Alternatively, cook well in advance and freeze, then freshen up in the oven for a few minutes on the day.
- Step 2 can be cooked up to 2 days in advance and either reheated or served at room temperature.
- Step 3 can be made up to 2 days in advance.

**This easy, rustic, wafer-thin pastry tart is perfect for entertaining, not least because it's simply an assembly job when required, and an excellent way of stretching beef fillet to feed a lot of people. Fillet tails are cheaper than the middle cut, too. Good as a starter, main course or part of a buffet, warm or at room temperature.**

1. Preheat the oven to 220°C. Unroll the pastry onto a baking sheet lined with silicone paper or baking parchment. Prick all over with a fork and place the sheet of paper it was wrapped in over the top, followed by another baking sheet. Cook for 7–10 minutes or until richly golden and crispy. (Turn over if not browning in the middle, cover and cook a little longer.) Press down hard on the top baking sheet to flatten the pastry further, then remove the sheet, plus the paper. Leave to cool.

2. Meanwhile, tuck the thin end of the fillet tail/s underneath, so they're the same thickness, and secure with string. Smear with a little olive oil and pouring salt. Heat a frying pan until very hot, then seal the fillet well on all sides – this should take 5–8 minutes. Transfer to a plate and leave to rest for 15–20 minutes (or leave to cool).

3. For the watercress mayonnaise, process the mayonnaise and watercress together, then add lime juice and seasoning to taste. Thin with a little warm water if necessary. Put into a serving bowl and set aside.

4. Transfer the pastry to a board, and spread thinly and evenly with onion chutney. Slice the beef thinly, tear each slice into manageable pieces and arrange on top of the chutney in a wavy pattern. Mix the rocket leaves with a smidge of olive oil, sea salt and black pepper, and scatter over the beef, followed by Pecorino shavings, a few capers and a final swirl of olive oil. Cut into the required number of slices and serve as is, or transfer to a serving platter, with the watercress mayonnaise.

### Hints & Tips

- Foaming Béarnaise, Romesco sauce (see page 120) and horseradish mayonnaise are delicious alternative sauces. Or use crème fraîche or plain yoghurt as a sauce base for different flavourings. Sometimes I like to blitz parsley and tarragon leaves into watercress mayo.
- A few roughly chopped, or sliced, pickled walnuts are very good nestled into the beef.
- A little quick pickled red onion is also very good strewn over the beef.
- Roasted baby beets are a lovely accompaniment to the beef.
- Baba Ganoush (see page 23) is a tasty alternative to the onion chutney.
- For fewer people, cut out individual tarts and keep the spare cooked pastry wrapped in clingfilm or freeze it until needed.

# SALMON, COURGETTI & ASPARAGUS WITH LIME & CAPER DRESSING

SERVES 4–6

**2 medium courgettes, spiralized**
**a bunch of asparagus (10–12 spears)**
**100g (3½oz) samphire (optional)**
**olive oil**
**4–6 skinless salmon fillets, 110–140g (4–5oz) each**
**sea salt**
**275g (10oz) fresh, cooked egg (or rice) noodles**
**cress or micro leaves, to garnish (optional)**

FOR THE DRESSING

**zest and freshly squeezed juice of 1 large lime**
**1 tbsp white wine vinegar**
**2 heaped tbsp capers, drained**
**1 clove of garlic, crushed**
**2 heaped tsp seedy mustard**
**5 tbsp olive oil**
**1 tsp salt**
**freshly ground black pepper**
**1 tbsp freshly chopped tarragon (or dill or coriander)**

### Get Ahead

Prepare steps 1–5 up to 2 days ahead, and step 6, if serving the salmon cold. Either way, do not add the tarragon to the dressing until the last minute.

**A burst of summery freshness – zingy, piquant and delicious – it's easy and quick to make, too. Keep it simple and eat as a light, quick lunch or supper, or dress it up to become a show-stopping prepare-ahead platter for entertaining numbers.**

1. Preheat the oven to 200°C. Mix together all the dressing ingredients, except for the tarragon, and set aside.

2. Blanch the courgettes in boiling salted water for just 30 seconds – no longer! Drain, cool and leave rolled up in kitchen paper to dry thoroughly.

3. Snap off and discard the woody asparagus ends and cook in well-salted boiling water for a few minutes until just tender. Drain and cool under cold water. Cut the spears in half, or thirds if very long.

4. Cook the samphire, if using, in boiling unsalted water for 3 minutes, drain and cool under cold water. Roll up in kitchen paper with the asparagus to dry.

5. Line a baking sheet with foil and lightly oil. Tuck the thin end of the salmon fillets underneath, so they are a more even thickness, and place onto the baking sheet.

6. Dribble a little olive oil and scatter some sea salt flakes over the fillets, and bake in the preheated oven for 5–6 minutes. The salmon should be opaque on the outside and still a little underdone in the middle.

7. Put the noodles into a large bowl and season. Add the courgettes, asparagus (reserving a few tips) and all but a handful of samphire, if using. Add the tarragon to the dressing and spoon 4 tablespoons into the noodles. Incorporate everything very gently – hands are best! Pile onto a platter, break the salmon into chunky flakes and nestle it over the top. Decorate with the reserved asparagus and samphire, and spoon over the rest of the dressing. Scatter with cress or micro leaves, if using.

### Hints & Tips

- Serve warm or at room temperature.
- Alternatively, scatter watercress over a platter, top with (warm or cold) halved baby new potatoes, then the vegetables. Arrange the salmon on top and spoon over some dressing. Or, serve the salmon fillets with new potatoes, green veg or salad and the dressing for an easy lunch or supper.
- You can use a 450g (1lb) piece of salmon fillet, cooked for 10 minutes wrapped in foil, then break into large flakes over the noodles.
- Add prawns or use instead of salmon. To butterfly raw, shelled prawns, halve the body lengthways, leaving 1cm (½in) of the tail end intact. Stir-fry in a little hot oil for 1–2 minutes.

# PEPPERED FRESH TUNA NIÇOISE

SERVES 4–6

300g (11oz) fine French beans, topped but not tailed
12 quail's eggs (or 4–5 hen's eggs)
mixed salad leaves, such as 1 small bag of baby spinach, 1 bag of mixed leaves and 1 round lettuce
450g (1lb) waxy new potatoes, cooked
½ a red onion, sliced very thinly
250g (9oz) cherry or baby plum tomatoes, halved
12–15 black olives, stoned
8 anchovy fillets, snipped into slivers
2 tbsp cracked black pepper
salt
2 x 225g (8oz) tuna steaks
olive oil
1 tsp tapenade

FOR THE DRESSING
½ tsp salt
1 tsp Dijon mustard
1 clove of garlic, crushed
2 tbsp red wine vinegar
7 tbsp olive oil
1 tbsp freshly chopped tarragon

**Fresh, vibrant and very savoury, this salad transports me straight to the Mediterranean. Perfect for even the hottest of days, with the added bonus that it can all be prepared the day before, ready for a last-minute assembly job minutes before devouring.**

1. Cook the beans in boiling salted water until just tender. Drain, cool under cold water and dry well on kitchen paper.

2. Bring the quail's eggs to the boil in a pan of water and cook for 2 minutes. Drain and cool under cold running water and peel, then submerge in a bowl of cold water.

3. Mix the dressing ingredients together.

4. Scatter the salad leaves over the bottom of a large platter, tearing any larger ones. Scatter over the beans. Cut the potatoes lengthways into three or so and halve the eggs. Arrange the potatoes over the beans, followed by the red onion, tomatoes and the halved eggs. Dot around the black olives and anchovies.

5. Heat a frying or griddle pan, until very hot. Spread the cracked pepper onto a plate; rub a little salt into the tuna steaks and then press into the pepper to coat. (Alternatively, grind pepper from a mill over the steaks.) Rub with a little olive oil and sear for about 30 seconds on each side. Slice diagonally and arrange over the salad. Spoon over the dressing. Mix the tapenade to a sauce consistency with some olive oil and dribble over the salad.

### Get Ahead

All the components, except for the tuna, can be prepared up to a day ahead and kept covered separately in the fridge. However, if not serving warm, the tuna can also be cooked a day ahead and sliced when required.

### Hints & Tips

- Dressing the salad 15 minutes or so before eating gives the flavours time to meld together.
- Use two tins of tuna, drained, instead of fresh, if you prefer.
- Very good with Tapenade Breadsticks (see page 34).

# RACK OF LAMB, FREEKEH, WALNUTS & TAPENADE CRUMBS

SERVES 6

a good handful of walnuts
1–2 tbsp runny honey
15g (½oz) dried breadcrumbs
2 tsp tapenade
olive oil
2 racks of lamb, chined and French-trimmed (14–16 cutlets)
Worcestershire sauce
200g (7oz) dried freekeh
300g (11oz) fine French beans, tops trimmed
100–125g (3–4oz) bag of baby spinach or watercress
1 small (or ½ a large) red onion, halved and finely sliced
a handful of black olives, pitted or not
2 sprigs of mint, leaves roughly chopped
2–3 tbsp pomegranate seeds
salt and freshly ground black pepper
baby cherry tomatoes on the vine, roasted (optional, see Hints & Tips, page 114)

FOR THE SAUCE
175g (6oz) natural Greek yoghurt
1 clove of garlic, crushed
2 tbsp olive oil
freshly squeezed juice of ½ a lemon
2 sprigs of mint, leaves chopped

### Get Ahead

The walnuts, tapenade crumbs, freekeh, beans and tomatoes, if using, can be cooked, and the sauce made, the day before. If serving the beans and freekeh warm, reheat individually in a saucepan in a little olive oil before slicing the lamb.

**A lovely prepare-ahead summer entertaining platter, which requires little effort. In the supermarket, you will find dried freekeh alongside other dried grains.**

1. Oil a baking sheet, or line with silicone paper. Mix the walnuts with just enough honey to coat them all. Cook the nuts in a frying pan, stirring over a high heat for a few minutes until golden and caramelized. Tip out and spread immediately onto the prepared baking sheet. Leave to cool.

2. Preheat the oven to 220°C. In a small bowl, mix together the breadcrumbs and tapenade. Heat a little olive oil in a pan, add the mixture and fry over a high heat for a few minutes until golden and crispy. Set aside in a small bowl.

3. Make the sauce by mixing all the ingredients together. If very thick, thin with a little water (although it shouldn't be too runny). Set aside.

4. Rub the skin of the lamb with a little Worcestershire sauce, put into a small, lightly oiled roasting tin and cook at the top of the oven for 15–20 minutes for pink lamb (cooking time will depend on the size of the racks – very large racks will need 20–25 minutes). Transfer from the roasting tin to a plate and leave somewhere warm to rest for a minimum of 20 minutes (but up to an hour or so is fine).

5. Meanwhile, cook the freekeh according to the pack instructions. Drain, season well, stir in a little olive oil and keep warm if using straightaway, or leave to cool. Cook the beans in boiling salted water until just tender, drain, refresh briefly under cold water and keep warm if using straightaway, or cool them under cold water and wrap in kitchen paper until needed.

6. Arrange the spinach or watercress around the edge of a large platter. Pile the freekeh into the middle, scatter over the French beans and then the red onion.

7. Slice the lamb into cutlets and arrange over the top with the bones standing up. Pour over any lamb juices. Trickle over a little of the yoghurt sauce and scatter with the walnuts, olives, mint, pomegranate seeds and, finally, the tapenade crumbs and a swirl of olive oil. Serve the rest of the sauce separately in a pretty bowl.

### Hints & Tips

- Allow 2–3 cutlets per person.
- The lamb should be served hot or warm; the rest of the ingredients can be warm or at room temperature.
- Or, the uncooked racks can be cut into individual cutlets and barbecued for a few minutes on each side until charred on the outside and pink in the middle. Coating them with dukkah first makes them even more delicious!

# STUFFED SHOULDER OF LAMB WITH CAPER SAUCE

SERVES 8

1 shoulder of lamb, boned

FOR THE STUFFING

olive oil
1 onion, chopped
4 rashers of streaky bacon, snipped into thin strips
2 cloves of garlic, crushed
2 sprigs of rosemary, leaves chopped
200g (7oz) chestnut mushrooms, chopped
250g (9oz) baby spinach, wilted, squeezed dry and roughly chopped
a handful of pine nuts, toasted
salt and freshly ground black pepper

FOR THE CAPER SAUCE

40g (1½oz) butter
40g (1½oz) plain flour
700ml (1¼ pint) milk, possibly more
3 tbsp small capers, plus their juice
a handful of spinach or wild garlic leaves, thinly shredded (optional)

### Get Ahead

Prepare to the end of step 2 up to a day ahead. The sauce (step 4) can be made up to 3 days in advance.

### Hints & Tips

Redcurrant sauce is a lovely alternative to caper sauce. Bring 4 tbsp redcurrant jelly, 4 tbsp red wine vinegar and 570ml (1pint) lamb or chicken stock (or 2 stock cubes) to the boil; simmer until reduced by about half. This can be made up to 4 days ahead, or frozen.

**A lovely roast for Sunday lunch and a great dish to serve at Easter. If your butcher is as friendly as mine and if you give them notice, they may happily incorporate your stuffing, then roll and tie the joint for you. Redcurrant sauce (see Hints & Tips, below left) is an alternative to caper sauce, in which case the Gratin Dauphinois (see page 136) would be a perfect accompaniment, individually cut out for an extra touch of elegance!**

1. Preheat the oven to 220°C. To make the stuffing, heat a little olive oil in a sauté pan, add the onion and bacon and cook slowly for about 10 minutes, stirring occasionally, until softened. Add the garlic, rosemary and mushrooms, and fry until all the liquid has evaporated. Add the spinach and pine nuts. Taste and season well. Tip onto a plate and spread out to cool.

2. Meanwhile, open out the shoulder, skin-side down, and trim off all excess fat. Butterfly any thicker fleshy bits by slashing and opening them out. When the stuffing is cold, spread over the meat, distributing it into all the nooks and crannies and fold the loose flaps back in, over the stuffing. Roll up tightly and secure with string, starting in the middle and working outwards equally and alternately along each side, at roughly 2.5–4cm (1–1½in) intervals (around eight ties in total). Then tie once along the length of the joint, tucking the string underneath the first middle tie, to gain grip and make it tight. Push any escaped stuffing back inside the joint.

3. Put the lamb into a roasting tin, rub with a little pouring salt and cook for 1 hour 5 minutes. Remove to a cold plate and leave to sit for 10 minutes to stop it cooking. Then keep it somewhere warm (such as the oven with the door ajar) to rest for a minimum of 30 minutes (45–60 minutes is better and longer is fine). Skim off the fat in the roasting tin and pour the juices into a little jug. Keep warm.

4. To make the sauce, melt the butter in a saucepan, stir in the flour to make a roux and cook for a minute. Gradually whisk in the milk and season with salt and pepper. Bring to the boil, stirring or whisking all the time, until thickened. Bubble for a few minutes, then add the capers with a little of their liquid. If the mixture is too thick, thin it down with a little more milk and bubble it up again. Cover the surface with greaseproof paper and set aside.

5. Just before serving, reheat the sauce, adding a little more milk, if necessary, to achieve a pouring consistency, and add any juices from the plate the lamb is resting on. Stir in the spinach or wild garlic leaves, if using, and transfer to a serving bowl or jug.

6. Slice the lamb and arrange on a platter, pour over the reserved pan juices and serve with the caper sauce.

# SALADS & SIDES

# GRATIN DAUPHINOIS

SERVES 6–8

900g (2lb) floury potatoes, such as Maris Piper
350ml (12fl oz) milk
150ml (5fl oz) double cream
1 clove of garlic, crushed
2 tsp salt
freshly ground black pepper
2 tbsp grated Parmesan cheese (see tip, page 10)

### Hints & Tips

Increase the quantities by one and a half times to feed 12 people. Double the quantities to feed 20 and allow 1½ hours to cook.

**This is the French method of cooking these classic creamy potatoes. The process begins in a saucepan, rather than the typically British way of piling potatoes into a dish and pouring cream over the top. Not only does this give a far superior result, it also uses hardly any cream. See Get Ahead (below) for how to make this entirely in advance and present it elegantly when entertaining.**

1. Preheat oven to 190°C. Butter a shallow ovenproof gratin dish measuring about 20 x 25cm (8 x 10in).

2. Peel and thinly slice the potatoes using a food processor, mandolin or knife. Do not put the sliced potatoes into water.

3. Put the milk, cream, garlic, seasoning and potatoes into a large pan and, using a wooden spoon, carefully mix together over a gentle heat, until the mixture becomes thick and creamy.

4. Pour into the greased dish and sprinkle the top with the grated Parmesan. Bake in the preheated oven for 1 hour or until the potatoes are very tender and the top is golden brown and bubbling. Check after 45–50 minutes to make sure the top isn't getting too brown. Keep an eye on it and cover loosely with foil if necessary.

### Get Ahead

- Make entirely up to 24 hours in advance, cool, cover and refrigerate. When required, reheat at the above temperature for 20–25 minutes, although it won't be quite as creamy as when freshly cooked.
- Alternatively, after a night in the fridge, and up to 2 days ahead, cut out 6–8 rounds with a plain pastry cutter, or chef's ring (around 7cm/2¾in across for 6 rounds; smaller for 8) and, using a palette knife, place on a baking sheet, greased or lined with silicone paper. Reheat at 200°C for 10–12 minutes when required (pictured). Or, cut the gratin into squares instead, which avoids any wastage.

# VIBRANT CRUNCHY WILD RICE SALAD WITH SHALLOT VINAIGRETTE

(V)

SERVES 6–8

100g (3½oz) tenderstem broccoli
100g (3½oz) sugar snap peas
250g (9oz) asparagus spears
2 spring onions, trimmed and sliced diagonally
125g (4½oz) (raw weight) wild rice, cooked (according to packet instructions), rinsed and dried
a handful of pumpkin seeds
a handful of hazelnuts, toasted and very roughly chopped
4 sprigs of mint, leaves roughly chopped
sunflower seeds, for sprinkling
a few radishes, with leaves if possible (optional)

FOR THE SHALLOT VINAIGRETTE

1 heaped tsp Dijon mustard
½ tsp salt
1 tbsp sherry vinegar
4 tbsp olive oil (or substitute 1 tbsp with hazelnut oil)
½ a shallot, finely chopped
1 small clove of garlic, crushed

**Fresh, crispy, crunchy, gluten-free, vegetarian and healthy! As well as being a great side dish, this salad can be dressed up as a delicious main course for lunch or supper. Very popular.**

1. Prepare the vegetables. Cut off and discard any fat, tough stems from the broccoli and roughly peel the remaining stems. String the sugar snap peas, if necessary, then cut in half diagonally. Gently bend the asparagus spears, snap off and discard the tough bottoms, then cut diagonally into two or three chunks (depending on their length).

2. Cook the vegetables in well-salted boiling water until just tender (the peas and asparagus can be cooked together). Drain and plunge straight into cold water. When cold, drain again and dry well, by spreading them out onto kitchen paper and rolling them up. Set aside.

3. Whisk all the vinaigrette ingredients together.

4. In a large bowl, gently amalgamate the vegetables and spring onions with the rice, pumpkin seeds, hazelnuts and three quarters of the mint, and then carefully stir through the vinaigrette. Pile into the middle of a serving plate or platter. Scatter over a few sunflower seeds and the rest of the mint, and garnish with radishes, if using.

### Get Ahead

Prepare steps 1–3 up to 24 hours ahead. The components of the salad can be amalgamated several hours in advance, but don't add the mint or dressing until the very last minute.

### Hints & Tips

- This can also be used as a base for any number of main courses: very good with roast salmon fillets, chicken or topped with a poached egg. A blob or two of Labneh (see page 24) alongside or on top is delicious, too.
- No need to stick rigidly to the vegetable quantities given above left – they are just a rough guide.
- Diced avocado is a possible addition that works very well.

(V)

# CHILLI-ROASTED TENDERSTEM BROCCOLI

SERVES 4

250g (9oz) tenderstem or purple sprouting broccoli
olive oil
sea salt
dried chilli flakes

### Get Ahead

Finish to the end of step 4 any time on the day, and reheat on the baking sheet for a few minutes, when required.

**Roasting tenderstem broccoli quickly in a hot oven until charred takes it to a whole new flavour level. It also retains its nutrients and bright green colour, and is a clever way of cooking veg in advance when entertaining. Enjoy it as a side, in a salad with toasted sesame seeds, with hollandaise sauce, or topped with a poached egg and grated Parmesan cheese.**

1. Preheat the oven to 220°C.

2. Cut the tough bottom sections off the broccoli stems, and roughly shave off the outer layer of the remaining stem with a knife. Split any thick stems in half, forming two 'trees'.

3. Spread the broccoli out onto a lightly greased baking tray in one layer. Dribble over a little olive oil, and sprinkle over some sea salt and a few chilli flakes.

4. Cook in the preheated oven for 10–15 minutes, depending on the size and thickness of the stems, until just tender and a little bit blackened and charred.

# PROVENÇAL TOMATOES

SERVES 6

**olive oil**
**900g (2lb) ripe tomatoes**
**4 cloves of garlic, chopped**
**a sprig or two of fresh oregano, or a good pinch of dried**
**a handful of dried breadcrumbs (see Hints & Tips, below right)**
**salt and freshly ground black pepper**

### Get Ahead

- Make up to 3 days in advance, cool, cover and refrigerate. Reheat in a moderate oven for 10–15 minutes. These tomatoes are very well behaved and impossible to overcook or spoil – unless, of course, you burn them!
- Alternatively, prepare to the end of step 4 at any time on the day and cook when required.

**These tomatoes are very popular in our household. In fact, so popular that I never seem to be able to make a large enough quantity and we rarely eat steak without them. This is a useful recipe to have in your repertoire as they are very versatile and can be made several days in advance.**

1. Preheat the oven to 220°C.

2. Grease a shallow ovenproof dish with a little olive oil. Cut the tomatoes into thickish slices and put a layer of them into the bottom of the dish.

3. Scatter with half of the garlic, a little oregano, and some salt, pepper and olive oil.

4. Repeat this with the rest of the tomatoes, garlic and seasoning, and finally scatter the breadcrumbs over the top. Swirl over a little more olive oil.

5. Roast in the preheated oven for 1–1¼ hours or until the tomatoes are very soft and well cooked. When properly cooked, the volume of the tomatoes will have reduced by half and all but a tablespoon or so of the now syrupy liquid will have evaporated, so they are almost dry. The cooking time will depend on the juiciness of the tomatoes.

### Hints & Tips

- Do use any variety of tomatoes, but they need to be as ripe as possible.
- Don't store tomatoes in the fridge as this impairs their flavour and prevents them from ripening.
- A good glug of double cream added towards the end of cooking lifts this into another league.
- It is very useful to have a stock of dried breadcrumbs. Simply spread old white bread and/or rolls out in a roasting tin and leave in a cooling oven until crisp and dry. Process until very fine and store them in a lidded container where they will last almost indefinitely. Try not to use too many dark crusts, as the crumbs need to be a white or pale biscuity colour. If they are too dark to begin with, they are likely to burn when cooked.

(V)

# ROASTED CRUSHED NEW POTATOES WITH ROSEMARY

SERVES 4–6

**1kg (2lb 4oz) small waxy new potatoes**
**salt**
**olive oil**
**2 sprigs of fresh rosemary, leaves chopped**
**sea salt**

### Get Ahead

Prepare to the end of step 3 up to 24 hours ahead. Cover and refrigerate.

### Hints & Tips

- Very good with cured and cold meats, griddled chicken and steaks, and the Tagliata (see page 114). In fact, with almost anything!
- Sometimes I like to put a little grated cheese on each potato and pop them back into the oven until melted and bubbling. Tapenade, chopped spring onions and/or herbs, fennel seeds, and persillade (garlic and parsley chopped together) all make delicious toppings.

**Positively irresistible, and the tastiest way of using up leftover new potatoes!**

1. Place the potatoes in a saucepan of cold, salted water, bring to the boil, then simmer until cooked and drain.

2. Preheat the oven to 220°C. Grease a shallow roasting tin or baking sheet, large enough to hold the potatoes in one layer, with a little olive oil.

3. Tip the potatoes into the tin and squash each one fairly flat with a potato masher or a fork. Some might break up a little, which is the nature of the beast and doesn't matter. Just press them back together.

4. Sprinkle over the chopped rosemary and some sea salt, followed by a good glug of olive oil. Roast in the preheated oven for 30–35 minutes or until golden brown and crispy.

Ⓥ

# BRAISED LEEKS WITH HERBS & PEAS

SERVES 4

**3 medium leeks, trimmed and washed**
**300ml (10fl oz) chicken or vegetable stock (or 1 stock cube)**
**225g (8oz) frozen petits pois**
**a handful of parsley leaves, chopped (a few tarragon, thyme or mint leaves would be good, too)**
**salt and freshly ground black pepper**

**Good with almost anything, especially fish, chicken and the Duck Confit (see page 110).**

1. Cut each leek diagonally into four equal pieces. Put into a sauté pan, which has a lid, pour in the stock, add some seasoning (no salt if using a stock cube) and bring to the boil. Cover and simmer very gently for 15–20 minutes until the leeks are very tender (but still holding their shape).

2. Add the frozen peas, bring back to the boil and check the seasoning. Simmer uncovered for 5 minutes or until the peas are just cooked but still bright green. Stir in half the parsley and other herbs, if using.

3. Remove from the stock with a slotted spoon and transfer to a serving dish. Scatter with the remaining parsley and other herbs, if using.

### Get Ahead

Make to the end of step 2 up to 24 hours in advance, but don't add the herbs until it's reheated.

### Hints & Tips

- If doubling up the recipe, you don't need to up the quantity of stock.
- This lends itself to the addition/substitution of almost any vegetable.

# CELERIAC, POTATO & APPLE GRATIN



SERVES 8 (GENEROUSLY)

**butter, for greasing**
**350g (12oz) celeriac, peeled and thinly sliced**
**350g (12oz) potatoes, peeled and thinly sliced**
**3 dessert apples, peeled, cored and thinly sliced**
**2 heaped tsp English mustard**
**300ml (10fl oz) crème fraîche or double cream**
**4 tbsp grated Parmesan cheese**
**1 tbsp dried breadcrumbs**
**salt and freshly ground black pepper**

**A very tasty accompaniment to hot or cold grilled and roasted meats and poultry, and particularly good with pork, ham and sausages. This always delivers a surprise, as it's not at all what it seems; delicious on its own or, if you use a vegetarian alternative to Parmesan, as part of a vegetarian feast.**

1. Preheat the oven to 200°C. Grease a shallow ovenproof dish with butter.

2. In a large bowl, mix together the sliced celeriac, potatoes and apples, seasoning well with salt and pepper. Tip into the prepared dish and even out the top.

3. Mix the mustard and crème fraîche or double cream together, season and pour over the celeriac mixture. Scatter the Parmesan cheese over the top, followed by the breadcrumbs.

4. Bake in the preheated oven for 1–1¼ hours or until the gratin is tender when pierced with a sharp knife. Check after 30–40 minutes to make sure the top isn't getting too brown. Keep an eye on it and cover loosely with foil if necessary.

### Get Ahead

- Prepare to the end of step 3 up to an hour or so in advance.
- Cook the gratin up to 2 days in advance and reheat when required.

### Hints & Tips

Very good at any time of year, but particularly when entertaining at Christmas as an accompaniment to all those cold meats. It cheers up cold turkey no end!

# SIZZLING SHREDDED SPROUTS WITH BACON & WALNUTS

SERVES 4–6

**340g (12oz) Brussels sprouts**
**6 rashers of streaky bacon, snipped into thin strips**
**olive oil**
**2 knobs of butter**
**a handful of walnuts, roughly chopped**
**walnut oil (optional)**
**salt and freshly ground black pepper**

### Get Ahead

- The sprouts can be shredded several days in advance and kept covered in the fridge.
- The bacon can be fried at any time on the day and left in the pan until you are ready to cook the sprouts.

**Perfect for converting sprout-haters (I have proof!). Easy, quick, vibrant, nutty and delicious!**

1. Slice off any brown bits from the base of the sprouts and shred them using the slicer blade of a food processor. Set aside.

2. Heat a wok or large frying pan and dry-fry the strips of bacon until golden and crispy.

3. Add a little olive oil and a good knob of butter to the pan and, when hot, add the sprouts, a handful at a time, and stir until they have just wilted and turned a vibrant bright green colour. Season generously, then remove from the heat, add the walnuts, an extra knob of butter and a swirl of walnut oil, if using. Serve immediately.

### Hints & Tips

- Roughly chopped salted peanuts would be a good alternative to walnuts, with (or without) a sprinkling of toasted sesame seeds.
- Vacuum-packed chestnuts crumbled into the sprouts at the last minute is another tasty alternative.
- This is very good as a side dish, on its own, or with a fried or poached egg on top. A trickle of sriracha sauce over the egg would round it off perfectly!

# KISIR

SERVES 4–6 AS A SALAD, OR MORE AS PART OF A MEZZE

olive oil
1 onion, finely chopped
1 tbsp tomato purée
1 tsp ground cumin
¼ tsp chilli flakes
½ tsp paprika
1 good tsp salt
freshly ground black pepper
200g (7oz) bulgur wheat
a handful of walnuts, roughly chopped
¼ cucumber, cut into small dice
4 spring onions, trimmed and chopped
a large handful of parsley, chopped, plus a few leaves for decoration
a large handful of mint, chopped
½ a bunch of dill, chopped

FOR THE DRESSING

1 tbsp pomegranate molasses (or balsamic vinegar)
freshly squeezed juice of ½ a lemon
1 tbsp olive oil

SERVING SUGGESTIONS

Pomegranate seeds, Greek yoghurt, Little Gem lettuce, pitta bread

**Kisir is the Turkish version of Middle Eastern tabbouleh and, like many classics the world over, it varies from region to region.**

1. Heat a little olive oil in a sauté pan, add the onion and cook gently until soft and translucent. Stir in the tomato purée, cumin, chilli flakes, paprika, salt and pepper. Cook for a minute or so, then add the bulgur wheat and 225ml (8fl oz) water. Bring to the boil, stir well, remove from the heat and cover with a lid. Leave for 10–15 minutes until the bulgur is cooked and has cooled a little.

2. Mix the dressing ingredients together and stir into the bulgur mixture. Check the seasoning – it will almost definitely need more salt.

3. Stir in the remaining ingredients if eating warm straightaway, or wait until cool before adding them if serving at room temperature. Pile onto a platter and decorate as you wish, finishing with a swirl of olive oil at the last minute.

### Get Ahead

Make to the end of step 2 up to 2 days ahead, adding the walnuts, cucumber and spring onions, but not the herbs until the day. Bring back to room temperature before eating. Any leftovers will last for several days in the fridge.

### Hints & Tips

Another traditional way of serving Kisir is spooned into individual Little Gem lettuce leaves, arranged on a large platter and scattered with pomegranate seeds. This quantity fills 30 or more Little Gem leaves.

(V)

# FRENCH BEANS WITH MUSHROOMS, GARLIC & PINE NUTS

SERVES 4–6

30g (1oz) butter, plus a little extra
250g (9oz) chestnut mushrooms, sliced fairly thinly
freshly squeezed juice of ½ a lemon
1 clove of garlic, crushed
400g (14oz) fine French beans
olive oil (optional)
a handful of pine nuts, toasted (optional)
salt and freshly ground black pepper

**This is a handy way of getting ahead on the vegetable front, especially when entertaining. Both tasty and savoury, these beans are particularly good with steak, as well as most other meat and fish.**

1. Melt the butter in a saucepan, add the mushrooms, season well and cook fast until nearly all the liquid has evaporated. Add the lemon juice and garlic, and cook until the mushrooms start sizzling and begin to turn golden brown. Set aside.

2. Meanwhile, cook the beans in well-salted boiling water for a few minutes until just tender. Drain and refresh quickly under the cold tap.

3. Reheat the mushrooms, add the beans and gently stir together over the heat, adding a little extra butter (or oil) if necessary. Add the pine nuts, if using, and serve.

### Get Ahead

Cook the mushrooms and beans up to 3 days in advance. Keep the mushrooms covered in a bowl in the fridge. When the beans are cooked, cool immediately in, or under, cold water. Drain, spread them out on kitchen paper and roll them up. Wrap or cover with clingfilm and keep in the fridge. When required, melt a little butter in a saucepan large enough to hold both ingredients. Heat the mushrooms first, then add the beans and pine nuts, and toss and mix very gently until heated through.

### Hints & Tips

Use any mushrooms you like, but they do need to be fresh, otherwise the black tinge that older ones have will spoil the colour of the dish.

# STIR-FRIED SAVOY CABBAGE, FIVE WAYS

(V)

SERVES 8

**1 medium Savoy cabbage, any tough outer leaves discarded**

**Get Ahead**
The cabbage can be shredded up to 3 days in advance and kept in the fridge in a polythene bag or covered in a bowl.

**Versatile cabbage can be served in myriad ways. The trick is to cook it quickly and not let it stew. Any other varieties of green cabbage can be used for the suggestions below.**

Cut the cabbage into quarters and remove the core from each quarter. Using a sharp chopping or bread knife, shred as finely as is humanly possible, lengthways, discarding any tough ribs along the way.

## BASIC RECIPE

Heat a little olive oil and/or butter in a wok or large saucepan and add the cabbage in batches, adding more as the previous batch begins to wilt. Season, and toss over a high heat, using a wooden spoon, until all the cabbage has just wilted. It should still be a bright translucent green. This will only take minutes.

## CRISPY BACON

Snip 4–6 rashers of streaky bacon into strips, dry-fry until crisp and continue as in the basic recipe.

## ASIAN

Toast a few white and/or black sesame seeds in a dry wok or large saucepan until fragrant. Remove and set aside. Cook the cabbage in a little toasted sesame oil, as in the basic recipe, then scatter with the sesame seeds.

## SPICE IT UP

Gently fry a scant teaspoon of caraway seeds in a little vegetable oil and/or butter until fragrant, add the cabbage and stir-fry as in the basic recipe.

## CREAMY MUSTARD CABBAGE

Stir-fry as in the basic recipe, adding 1–2 teaspoons of seedy mustard and a dollop or two of crème fraîche or double cream at the end. Bubble up until thickened a little, then serve. This is especially good with ham, pork and sausages.

# SWISS CHARD & GRUYÈRE GRATIN

SERVES 4–6

**700g (1lb 9oz) Swiss chard**
**olive oil**
**250ml (9fl oz) double cream**
**1 heaped tsp Dijon mustard**
**freshly squeezed juice of ½ a lemon**
**85g (3oz) Gruyère cheese, grated**
**2 tbsp dried breadcrumbs**
**salt and freshly ground black pepper**

**Chard is one of the most bountiful and rewarding vegetables we grow at home, producing an almost year-round supply. We grow a variety called Bright Lights, the stems of which have a beautiful, dazzling jewel-like colour spectrum and look pretty edging the beds in the veg garden. Like all things green and leafy, it's very good for you.**

1. Preheat the oven to 200°C.

2. Chop the stems off the chard and cut into 2.5cm (1in) chunks, wash well and drain. Stack the leaves into piles with the larger leaves at the bottom, roll up into tight cigarette shapes and slice into fine ribbons. Wash and drain but keep separate from the stems.

3. Heat a little olive oil in a large saucepan or wok and add the stems. Stir-fry for about 5 minutes or until beginning to soften. Add the leaves a handful at a time, season and stir until wilted. This will only take a few minutes. Tip into a sieve and leave to drain.

4. Meanwhile, pour the cream into the pan, season with a little salt and pepper, bring to the boil and bubble fast for 2–3 minutes until really quite thick (it needs to be thick, as liquid from the chard will thin it out later). Stir in the Dijon mustard and lemon juice.

5. Gently squeeze the excess moisture from the chard, return to the pan and mix together. Check the seasoning and tip into a shallow ovenproof gratin dish. Scatter the cheese and dried breadcrumbs over the top and bake in the preheated oven for 10–15 minutes until golden brown and bubbling.

### Get Ahead

Prepare entirely in advance at any time on the day, or cook steps 2–4 the day before and amalgamate on the day.

### Hints & Tips

A very good accompaniment to beef, game, chicken, ham or fish, as well as a delicious meal in itself, with some bread for mopping purposes and a green salad.

# FATTOUSH

(V)

SERVES 6–8

2 pitta breads
olive oil
340g (12oz) ripe tomatoes (regular, cherry or a mixture)
½ a cucumber
110–140g (4–5oz) radishes (about 12 in total), thinly sliced
4 spring onions, trimmed and thinly sliced diagonally
a handful of parsley, leaves chopped
a handful of mint, leaves chopped
1 small cos lettuce (or ½ a large one), sliced into ribbons

FOR THE DRESSING

½ tbsp sumac, plus extra for dusting
freshly squeezed juice of ½ a lemon
½ tbsp pomegranate molasses
2 tbsp olive oil
1 clove of garlic, crushed
¾ tsp salt

**An easy and very delicious Lebanese salad. Crisp, lemony, zingy and sharp, as well as refreshing and healthy – and a good way of using up stale pitta bread. Fattoush goes with almost anything and is delicious on its own, too. Use the freshest, ripest ingredients and treat this recipe as a guide only, adding or subtracting any ingredients you like or just whatever you have to hand. And that goes for quantities, too.**

1. Cut the pitta breads in half and then split open horizontally. Cut or tear into small bite-sized pieces. Heat a little olive oil in a frying pan and fry the pittas until golden and crispy. Drain on kitchen paper and set aside.

2. Cut the tomatoes and cucumber into bite-sized chunks and put into a large bowl with the radishes and spring onions, followed by the herbs.

3. Mix all the dressing ingredients together.

4. Just before serving, add the lettuce and most of the pitta crisps to the salad, reserving a few for decoration. Add the dressing and mix together. Check the seasoning and spoon into a shallow pretty bowl or onto a platter. Finish off with the reserved pitta crisps, a swirl of olive oil and a sprinkling of sumac.

**Get Ahead**

The dressing can be made 2 days in advance. The salad ingredients and herbs can be prepared several hours in advance but don't amalgamate the components, or dress the salad, until the last minute.

**Hints & Tips**

- If you prefer, the pitta pieces can be baked without oil in the oven.
- I sometimes decorate this salad with whole radishes, complete with their leaves.

# CELERIAC RÉMOULADE

SERVES 8

1 small or ½ a large celeriac, roughly 450g (1lb)
6–8 tbsp good, thick mayonnaise
2 tbsp seedy mustard or seedy honey mustard
2 tbsp Dijon mustard
salt and freshly ground black pepper

**Celeriac Rémoulade makes an excellent salad accompaniment to cold meats, a tasty starter (see Hints & Tips, below right) and is a traditional part of a platter of crudités. It is also delicious alongside rich casseroles and stews, such as Braised Oxtail (see page 86), and good with Duck Confit (see page 110).**

1. Cut a thin slice off the bottom of the celeriac, sit it on a chopping board and remove the skin using a large, sharp knife. Chop the flesh into thick chunks and grate using a food processor or a mandolin, or cut into matchsticks by hand.

2. Put into a mixing bowl and stir in the mayonnaise, a little at a time, as you may not need it all. Stir in the mustards and check the seasoning.

### Get Ahead

The rémoulade will sit happily in the fridge, covered, for a week.

### Hints & Tips

As a starter, spoon a small mound of celeriac into the middle of individual plates, arrange two slices of Parma ham around each one in a wavy pattern. Place a little scrunch of watercress, a few caperberries or a fanned-out gherkin or two on top of the celeriac mounds, then scatter with capers. Delicious served with griddled bread (see page 22).

# COURGETTE TIAN

SERVES 8–10

1kg (2lb 4oz) courgettes, trimmed and sliced 5mm (¼in) thick
olive oil
butter
1 onion, finely chopped
1 clove of garlic, crushed
70g (2½oz) (raw weight) basmati rice, cooked
a good handful of parsley, finely chopped
85g (3oz) Gruyère cheese, grated
1 tbsp dried breadcrumbs
salt and freshly ground black pepper

**This delicious classic French Provençal dish is an excellent way of using up a glut of courgettes. It stands up very well as a main course in its own right and as an accompaniment to meat, poultry, fish and anything barbecued.**

1. Preheat the oven to 220°C. Grease a shallow ovenproof dish.

2. Cook the courgettes in a saucepan of well-salted boiling water for only a minute or two, until just tender. Drain and refresh under cold water. Remove the excess moisture by spreading them out on kitchen paper, covering them with another sheet or two and rolling them up. Leave until required.

3. Heat a little olive oil and butter in a frying pan and gently cook the onion, with a pinch of salt, until soft. Add the garlic and cook for a minute longer.

4. Carefully mix together the onion and garlic, courgettes, cooked rice, parsley and roughly half of the cheese. Check the seasoning – it should be very well seasoned. Tip into the prepared ovenproof dish, and scatter over the remaining cheese and the breadcrumbs.

5. Bake for 15–20 minutes or until golden brown. Swirl with a little olive oil before serving.

### Get Ahead

Prepare to the end of Step 4 up to a day ahead. Cool, cover and refrigerate. Bring back to room temperature before cooking. It may take a little longer than 20 minutes to cook. Alternatively, complete the recipe entirely and reheat when required.

### Hints & Tips

For a richer, more luxurious version, a little double cream can be poured over the mixture before the final cheese topping.

# AUBERGINE WITH FETA, POMEGRANATE & CASHEW & CORIANDER PESTO

(V)

SERVES 8

**3 large or 4 medium aubergines**
**sea salt (smoked if you have it)**
**olive oil**
**1 tbsp natural yoghurt**
**110g (4oz) feta cheese**
**3–4 tbsp pomegranate seeds (approximately 40–50g/1½–2oz)**

FOR THE CASHEW & CORIANDER PESTO

**30g (1oz), or 2 good handfuls, coriander, tough stems removed**
**50g (2oz) plain cashew nuts, toasted**
**1 clove of garlic, roughly chopped**
**¼ tsp salt**
**6 tbsp olive oil**

**A wonderfully vibrant and flavourful platter that is a feast for the eyes, too. Just as good served as a starter or vegetarian main course. The pesto is also delicious with fish.**

1. Preheat the oven to 220°C.

2. Slice the aubergines widthways, on a diagonal, about 1cm (½in) thick. Arrange on a lightly oiled baking sheet in one layer. Scatter with sea salt and lightly drizzle with olive oil. Cook in the preheated oven for 10–15 minutes or until deep golden brown, and possibly a little bit charred, on the underside. Turn over and repeat with the other side, although this will take less time. Leave to cool. Arrange the slices, overlapping, on a large serving platter or on individual plates.

3. Meanwhile, reserving a few sprigs of coriander for decoration, make the pesto by processing all the ingredients, except the olive oil, together until amalgamated but still a little chunky. Pour in the olive oil, adding more if you prefer a slightly sloppier consistency.

4. In a ramekin, mix the yoghurt with ½ tablespoon of olive oil, a little salt and a splash of water, to loosen it.

5. Crumble the feta cheese over the aubergine, dribble over little spoonfuls of pesto, scatter with pomegranate seeds and swirl artistically with the yoghurt (or serve on the side). Finish with a swirl of olive oil and garnish with the reserved sprigs of coriander.

### Get Ahead

Prepare to the end of step 4 up to 2 days in advance. Cover individually and refrigerate. Bring back to room temperature at least an hour before eating. Step 5 can be completed 2–3 hours in advance but leave the yoghurt, olive oil and garnish till just before serving.

### Hints & Tips

Look for feta cheese that displays PDO on the packet. There are a lot of inferior imposters out there, so avoid labelling such as 'Greek Style Feta' or 'Greek Cheese', as these are not the real deal.

# · SWEET · THINGS

# LIME & COCONUT PANNA COTTA WITH MANGO PURÉE & PISTACHIOS

SERVES 8

**400ml (14fl oz) tin of coconut milk**
**400ml (14fl oz) double cream**
**5 tbsp caster sugar**
**3 limes**
**4 leaves of gelatine**
**1 ripe mango or 1 x 400g (14oz) tin of mango in syrup or mango pulp**
**½–1 tbsp icing sugar**
**a few pistachios, roughly chopped**

**These delicious panna cottas are very easy to make and convert even non-pudding eaters to the 'dark' side! Don't be put off by the leaf gelatine, as it is very user-friendly and this quantity produces just the right amount of wobble. For vegetarians, use agar-agar as a setting agent instead.**

**1.** Put the coconut milk, cream and sugar into a milk pan. Gently bring to the boil, stirring occasionally, and simmer for a minute or two. Add the zest of one, and the juice of 1½ limes. Pour into a jug and set aside while you prepare the gelatine.

**2.** Submerge the gelatine leaves in a bowl of cold water and leave for 5 minutes to soften. Remove from the water, squeeze out any excess liquid and stir the leaves into the still-warm cream mixture. Pour into 8 mini pudding moulds, ramekins or other small dishes, or pretty glasses. Cool, cover and refrigerate until set (preferably overnight).

**3.** Peel the mango, slice the flesh from the stone and reserve two slices. Process the rest into a purée with the icing sugar to taste. Cover and refrigerate. If using tinned mango, strain and then purée the flesh, adding icing sugar to taste.

**4.** To serve, if turning out, dip the moulds briefly into a bowl of hot water or loosen around the edges with your finger, creating a vacuum down to the base, and turn out onto individual plates. Dice the reserved mango and serve separately or arrange with a little purée around each panna cotta. Scatter with the pistachios, and grate a dusting of zest from the final lime over each plate. If serving in glasses, flood the tops with a little mango purée and decorate with the pistachios and lime zest.

**Get Ahead**

- Make to the end of step 2 up to 3 days in advance.
- Step 3 can be prepared at any time on the day.

**Hints & Tips**

- Use a milk-type saucepan, not non-stick, for the coconut milk and cream to avoid scorching.
- Substitute passion fruit or fresh berries for the mango.

# EASY HOT CHOCOLATE SOUFFLÉS WITH CHOCOLATE & CARDAMOM SAUCE

Ⓥ

MAKES 6

**butter, for greasing (spreadable butter is handy for this)**
**1 tbsp caster sugar, plus extra for dusting**
**100g (3½oz) plain chocolate, minimum 70% cocoa solids**
**200ml (7fl oz) good-quality ready-made vanilla custard**
**4 egg whites**
**pinch of salt**
**icing sugar, for dusting**

### Get Ahead

The soufflés can be made the day before up to the end of step 4, cooled, covered and kept in the fridge. Bring back to room temperature an hour or so before cooking. If making in advance on the day, they don't need to be refrigerated.

### Hints & Tips

- Add another tablespoon of sugar to the egg whites for sweeter soufflés.
- Serve with double cream instead of chocolate sauce. A few fresh berries on the side would be good, too.
- These also work as twice-baked soufflés. After cooking, and up to 2 days ahead, leave to cool and then turn out. Store covered on a plate or tray in the fridge. Place on a greased baking sheet or ovenproof dish(es), crust-side down, and cook as in step 5.

**These little soufflés are failsafe and ideal for impressing your guests, with no anxiety on your part. Just pop them into the oven after the main course and hey presto!**

1. Preheat the oven to 220°C. Grease 6 125–150ml (4–5fl oz) ramekins with butter, coat with caster sugar, then turn upside-down and tap hard to remove any excess sugar. Place on a baking sheet and set aside.

2. Gently melt the chocolate in a large bowl placed over a pan of hot water. Place the custard in a pan and warm through (do not boil), then stir into the chocolate.

3. Whisk the egg whites with a pinch of salt until they are stiff. Add 1 tablespoon of caster sugar and whisk again to incorporate. Stir a generous spoonful into the chocolate mixture to soften it, and then carefully fold in the rest of the egg whites.

4. Divide the mixture between the ramekins. Run your thumb or the point of a sharp knife around the edge of the mixture. This helps it to rise and form a 'hat'.

5. Bake in the preheated oven for 8–10 minutes, or until puffed up and well risen. Dust with icing sugar and serve immediately with the hot chocolate sauce (see below), handed separately or with a little poured into a hole, made with a spoon, in the middle of the soufflés.

## HOT CHOCOLATE & CARDAMOM SAUCE

**3 cardamom pods**
**100g (3½oz) plain chocolate, minimum 70% cocoa solids**
**150ml (5fl oz) whipping cream**
**½ tbsp golden syrup**
**a knob of butter**
**1 tsp strong black coffee**

1. Crack the cardamom pods under a heavy knife to release the seeds. Discard the husks and crush the seeds to a powder with a pestle and mortar.

2. Break the chocolate into pieces, put in a small pan with the cardamom and the rest of the ingredients, and stir over a very low heat until melted.

3. Serve in a jug or make a hole in the top of the soufflés and pour in.

### Get Ahead

Make up to 3 days in advance, cool, cover and refrigerate. Gently reheat when required.

### Hints & Tips

- Any leftover cold sauce can be used as chocolate spread. Add a few chopped hazelnuts if you like.
- Delicious poured over vanilla ice cream or profiteroles, too.
- Leave out the cardamom if you prefer.

(V)

# BAKED APRICOTS WITH PISTACHIOS, ROSEWATER & RICOTTA

SERVES 6

**140g (5oz) granulated sugar**
**1 vanilla pod, cut in half and split lengthways**
**1–2 tbsp rosewater**
**675g (1½lb) fresh apricots (approximately 10), halved and stoned**
**110g (4oz) ricotta cheese**
**honey, for drizzling**
**a handful of pistachios, slivered or chopped**

**A heavenly combination!**

**1.** Preheat the oven to 180°C.

**2.** Make a sugar syrup. Put the sugar and vanilla pod into a saucepan with 150ml (5fl oz) water. Heat, stirring gently, until the sugar has dissolved. Bring to the boil, then simmer for 5 minutes. Add 1 tbsp of rosewater.

**3.** Meanwhile, arrange the apricot halves in one layer in a shallow ovenproof dish into which they fit fairly snugly, stoned-side up. Spoon over the syrup, including the vanilla pieces, and cook in the preheated oven until soft, but still holding their shape. The cooking time will depend on how ripe the apricots are, so check after 15 minutes and then keep checking fairly regularly; they should be just soft when pierced with a sharp knife. Taste and add more rosewater if you think it needs it.

**4.** Leave to cool until warm, rather than hot, then spoon a little ricotta into the cavity of each apricot half. Drizzle with a little honey, scatter over the pistachio nuts and serve. If eating cold, cool then cover and refrigerate until required.

### Get Ahead

- Make to the end of step 3 up to 3 days in advance. Cool, cover and chill until required.
- If eating warm, reheat a little, before continuing with step 4.

### Hints & Tips

- The apricots can overcook and collapse very quickly, so beware.
- Delicious for breakfast, but you might like to swap the ricotta for some natural Greek yoghurt and eat them cold. They're also very good with porridge, granola and overnight oats.

(V)

# LEMON & RASPBERRY SHORTBREAD TORTE

SERVES 8–10

**170g (6oz) butter, at room temperature**
**85g (3oz) caster sugar**
**zest of 1 lemon**
**170g (6oz) plain flour**
**85g (3oz) cornflour**
**1 x 250g (9oz) tub of mascarpone cheese**
**4 tbsp good-quality lemon curd**
**675g (1½lb) fresh raspberries, or more if you like**
**icing sugar**

TO SERVE

**Edible dried rose petals, sprigs of mint and double cream (optional)**

### Get Ahead

- Make to the end of step 2 up to a week ahead and store in a cool place tightly wrapped in clingfilm, or make weeks in advance and freeze.
- Step 3 can be prepared up to 2 days ahead, covered and refrigerated.
- The torte can be assembled 3–4 hours in advance without going at all soggy. However, decorate just before serving.

**Fresh, pretty and ideal for summer entertaining, not least because everything can be prepared well in advance. Any other seasonal soft fruit or berries would be just as good, making the torte a flexible pudding for any time of year.**

**1.** Preheat the oven to 170°C.

**2.** Blitz the first five ingredients together briefly in a processor, until just amalgamated. Form the dough into a ball and knead gently with a little flour just until smooth. Do not overwork it. On a sheet of silicone paper, roll the dough out into a flat disc roughly 5mm (¼in) thick. Cut out a 24cm (9½in) circle. (Use any shortbread trimmings to make smaller biscuits.) Carefully slide the paper onto a baking sheet and chill for 15 minutes. Bake in the preheated oven for 20–25 minutes or until a very pale golden colour. (The biscuits will take less cooking time.) Allow to cool completely on the paper.

**3.** Beat together the mascarpone and lemon curd, adding more lemon curd to taste, if necessary (I sometimes use a whole jar).

**4.** Slide the shortbread onto a large flat plate. Spread the lemon curd mixture over the top, leaving a rim around the edge. Either arrange the raspberries over the top, or heap them up randomly. Before serving, dust with icing sugar and scatter with a few rose petals and/or tiny sprigs of mint, if using. Serve with cream on the side, if using.

# CARAMELIZED APPLE CREAMS

Ⓥ

MAKES 8

**1kg (2lb 4oz) cooking apples**
**140g (5oz) caster sugar**
**a good pinch of ground cinnamon**
**300ml (10fl oz) crème fraîche (you might not need it all)**
**demerara or soft brown sugar**

TO DECORATE
**Cape gooseberries (physalis, optional)**

**These popular little pots always prompt murmurs of surprise and delight. The crème brûlée-style topping belies the tart, fresh and clean apple found below.**

**1.** Peel, core and slice the apples, and cook in a pan with the caster sugar, cinnamon and a dribble of water over a gentle heat. Give them the odd stir and cook until the apple has completely collapsed and become a thick, translucent purée. Taste and add more sugar if necessary, bearing in mind it should be a little tart. Leave to cool.

**2.** Divide the apple between 8 ramekins or small pots, leaving quite a generous gap at the top. Chill thoroughly in the fridge.

**3.** Carefully spread the crème fraîche over the apple purée, covering completely and levelling the top. Chill again in the fridge until the crème fraîche is thoroughly cold. (This allows the sugar to caramelize in step 5 without melting the cream.)

**4.** Sprinkle a thin even layer of brown sugar over the crème fraîche (about 1 level dessertspoon per pot).

**5.** Using a cook's blowtorch or a grill preheated to its highest setting, caramelize the sugar to a crisp, deep golden-brown brûlée topping.

**6.** Return the pots to the fridge, uncovered, until completely cold before serving. Decorate with cape gooseberries, if using.

### Get Ahead

- Prepare to the end of step 2 up to 4 days in advance, or freeze the purée in one container.
- Complete to the end of step 3 up to 24 hours ahead.

### Hints & Tips

- The topping will stay crisp for an hour or two after caramelizing. Keep in the fridge, uncovered.
- In total, the recipe requires 550g (1lb 4oz) of apple purée.

(V)

# RUSTIC PEACH, RASPBERRY & ALMOND GALETTE WITH CRUSHED AMARETTI

SERVES 6–8

**½ a 500g (1lb 2oz) block of shortcrust pastry (or see Hints & Tips, below right)**
**170g (6oz) ready-to-roll marzipan**
**6 small or 4 large ripe peaches or nectarines (or 2 x 400g/14oz tins of peaches in syrup, well drained)**
**150g (5½oz) fresh raspberries**
**a knob of butter, melted**
**demerara sugar**

TO DECORATE

**Icing sugar, amaretti biscuits, edible dried or fresh rose petals, chopped pistachios (optional)**

TO SERVE

**Crème fraîche flavoured with Amaretto, to taste**

**Rustic and free-form, this is an easy and quick-to-make seasonal tart. It will turn out differently every time you make it, and pretty much any fruit, or fruit combinations, can be used.**

**1.** Preheat the oven to 200°C. Line a baking sheet with silicone or baking paper.

**2.** Roll the pastry into a circle roughly 38cm (15in) across. It doesn't have to be perfect by any means – wobbly edges add to the rustic charm! Transfer to the baking sheet.

**3.** Using the coarsest side of a box grater, grate the marzipan over the pastry, leaving a 5cm (2in) rim around the edges. Cut the peaches in half, discard the stone and slice into segments. Pile up on top of the marzipan in the middle of the pastry and scatter the raspberries over the top, nestling them into the peaches.

**4.** Bring the margins of the pastry up over the outside edges of the filling, leaving most of the fruit showing, pleating the edges over and over each other, forming a wavy effect. It needs a bit of height to hold the filling in during cooking. Brush the crimped pastry rim with melted butter, spooning any leftover butter over the fruit. Sprinkle the fruit lightly with demerara sugar, then dredge it more generously over the pastry rim. Chill for 20–30 minutes or until required.

**5.** Bake in the preheated oven for 20–25 minutes, or until golden and bubbling. It doesn't matter if some of the filling spills out – it's not meant to look perfect and this will depend on the ripeness and water content of the fruit. Cool for 15 minutes or so on the baking sheet, before sliding onto a serving plate or board.

**6.** Just before serving, dust with icing sugar and scatter with a few roughly crushed amaretti biscuits, dried or fresh rose petals and chopped pistachios, if using. Serve with Amaretto-flavoured crème fraîche. If serving warm, allow to sit for at least 20–30 minutes before eating. Serve warm or at room temperature, not piping hot.

### Get Ahead

Prepare to the end of step 4 at any time on the day, or to the end of step 5 up to 2 days ahead, and reheat a little or serve at room temperature. You may like to leave the tart on the baking sheet after cooking if you intend to warm it before serving.

### Hints & Tips

Rather than buying a block of pastry, use a ready-rolled shortcrust pastry disc.

# BAKED AMERICAN HONEYCOMB CHEESECAKE

(V)

SERVES 12–16

**55g (2oz) butter, melted**
**150g (5½oz) ginger nut biscuits (15 in number)**
**600g (1lb 5oz) cream cheese**
**110g (4oz) caster sugar**
**1 tsp plain flour**
**zest of 1 lemon**
**3 eggs**
**450ml (15fl oz) sour cream**
**1½ tsp vanilla extract**
**30g (1oz) white chocolate**
**fresh blackberries (optional)**
**(See Hints & Tips, below right, for more serving suggestions)**

FOR THE HONEYCOMB
**100g (3½oz) granulated sugar**
**2½ tbsp golden syrup**
**1 tsp bicarbonate of soda**

### Get Ahead

- Make to the end of step 3 up to 3 days in advance.
- Step 4 can be made several days in advance and kept in an airtight container. You will need to break the honeycomb up a bit first. It will last for several weeks.
- Step 5 can be done at any time on the day, but don't top with honeycomb and chocolate until the last minute.

**This is a heavenly combination of all the good things! Honeycomb is delicious dipped into melted chocolate so I often make extra for presents.**

**1.** Preheat the oven to 160°C. Line the base of a 23–24cm (9–9½in) springform tin with a square of baking paper, leaving the excess sticking out from the sides. Brush the inside of the tin with a little of the melted butter.

**2.** Process the biscuits into crumbs and stir into the rest of the butter. Press into the bottom of the tin, using the base of a flat glass for even distribution and for getting into the edges. Cook in the preheated oven for 15 minutes. Leave the oven on.

**3.** Meanwhile, process the cream cheese, sugar, flour and lemon zest together briefly, just until amalgamated. Add the eggs, one at a time, pulsing briefly and scraping the mixture down the sides of the bowl between each addition. Add 300ml (10fl oz) of the sour cream and the vanilla extract, and process again briefly. Pour into the prepared tin, put onto a baking sheet and cook for 45 minutes. The cheesecake will still be wobbly in the middle. Turn the oven off and leave the cheesecake in the cooling oven for an hour. Run a palette knife around the edge, cool completely, cover and refrigerate overnight.

**4.** To make the honeycomb, line a shallow tin or baking sheet with a sheet of silicone paper, or grease well. Dissolve the sugar and syrup together in a heavy-based, high-sided saucepan over a low heat. Give it the occasional gentle stir to help dissolve the sugar. Once it has dissolved, turn up the heat and bubble until it has turned a deep caramel colour – this will take around 5 minutes. Remove from the heat and stir in the bicarbonate of soda. It will froth up alarmingly! Quickly pour as thinly as possible onto the prepared tin. Set aside to cool.

**5.** To serve, melt the white chocolate in a small bowl or cup. Loosen the cheesecake with a palette knife, unclip the tin and transfer to a serving plate. Spread the top with the rest of the sour cream and drizzle with dulce de leche, if using (see below). Roughly break the honeycomb into assorted-sized chunks. *Just before serving,* pile them on top of the cheesecake and, using a teaspoon, drizzle with white chocolate (stir in a little vegetable oil if it's too thick). Tumble over a few blackberries, if using.

### Hints & Tips

- Drizzle a little thinned-down dulce de leche, or caramel spread, over the cheesecake, before the honeycomb.
- Don't worry if the top cracks during cooking, as it'll be covered up.
- **Alternative toppings:** Berry jam, stirred to loosen it, swirled into the sour cream with fresh berries piled on top; compotes, such as rhubarb, blueberry or black cherry; red berry coulis; pouring cream.

# PORTUGUESE CUSTARD TARTS (PASTÉIS DE NATA)

(V)

MAKES 12

**butter, for greasing**
**110g (4oz) caster sugar**
**2 tbsp cornflour**
**3 egg yolks**
**225ml (8fl oz) double cream**
**175ml (6fl oz) milk**
**2 tsp vanilla extract**
**1 sheet of ready-rolled all-butter puff pastry**
**ground cinnamon, for dusting**
**icing sugar, for dusting**

## Get Ahead

- Make the custard (step 2) up to 3 days ahead and keep in the fridge. Prepare to the end of step 4 at any time on the day.
- The tarts can be made several days ahead and eaten warmed through or at room temperature. You can't beat them freshly made but, though not ideal, they can be frozen; after thawing, freshen them up in a medium oven.

**Easy, easy, easy and beyond delicious! Enjoy these little delights at any time of day, any mealtime and for picnics, too.**

**1.** Grease a 12-hole muffin tin (this isn't necessary for non-stick tins).

**2.** In a saucepan, mix together the caster sugar, cornflour and egg yolks. Gradually add the cream and milk, whisking until smoothish. Don't worry about lumps – they will whisk out. Stir over a medium heat until the mixture becomes very thick and, just before it comes to the boil, stop whisking, remove from the heat, stir in the vanilla extract and then tip into a bowl. Cover with clingfilm placed directly on the custard, to prevent a skin from forming. Set aside to cool.

**3.** Preheat the oven to 200°C.

**4.** Unroll the pastry with the long edge closest to you (landscape), dust with a little cinnamon and cut in half vertically. Put one piece on top of the other and, starting from the bottom, shortest edge, roll it up tightly into a sausage shape. Slice into 12 even-sized discs. Roll out the discs, or flatten them into thin circles working with your fingers. Press them into the muffin tin and spoon the cold custard into the pastry cases.

**5.** Bake in the preheated oven for 20–25 minutes until the pastry is golden and the custard is puffed up, bubbling and golden in parts. Cool for 10 minutes before removing from the tin. (They will shrink down as they cool.) Caramelize with a cook's blowtorch if they're not as coloured as you would like. Sometimes they are, sometimes they're not! Serve either warm or at room temperature with a last-minute dusting of icing sugar and ground cinnamon.

# BLACK CHERRY, CHOCOLATE & MERINGUE ICE CREAM CAKE

Ⓥ

SERVES 12–16

**100g (3½oz) dark chocolate**
**390g (14oz) jar of black cherries in kirsch or 400g (14oz) tin of black cherries in syrup**
**250g (9oz, or 10 tbsp) black cherry conserve or jam**
**600ml (1 pint) double cream**
**85g (3oz) meringue nests (5–6 in number)**

TO SERVE
**Fresh cherries (with stalks), a handful of chopped pistachios, icing sugar**

### Get Ahead

- Make to the end of step 4 up to a month ahead. Remove from the tin at any time once it's frozen and wrap in clingfilm to store. Step 6 can be done at any time in advance, but it will take up more freezer space, and don't freeze the cherries or pistachios. The syrup will keep for a month in the fridge or longer in the freezer.
- The cake can be sliced in advance, arranged attractively on a platter and refrozen. In this case, drizzle the chocolate once the slices are arranged, and not over the cake as a whole. This is also a good way of representing a half-eaten/leftover cake – no one will know!

**The ultimate prepare-ahead summer pudding, and an inexpensive way of feeding a lot of people. It makes a lovely birthday cake, too!**

**1.** Line the base of a 23–24cm (9–9½in) springform tin with a square piece of baking paper, leaving the excess sticking out from the sides.

**2.** Melt the chocolate in a small bowl suspended over a pan of boiling water. Drain the cherries in a sieve set over a small saucepan to retain the kirsch or syrup. Roughly process or chop the cherries into a chunky, textured pulp. Stir the conserve or jam in a small bowl to loosen it.

**3.** In a food mixer or large mixing bowl, whip the cream until just beginning to thicken and barely holding its shape – the trick is to underwhip! Pour in the conserve, followed by the meringues, breaking and crumbling into irregular shapes and sizes as you go. Then fold into the cream very loosely and gently, leaving a ripple effect.

**4.** Spread a scant third of the mixture in the tin. Top with the chopped cherries by spooning them onto the cream in blobs, then joining the blobs. Spread over half of the remaining cream using the same technique; dribble over all but 2–3 tsp of the melted chocolate and spread to cover the cream. Finally, blob and spread over the last of the cream. Using a spatula or the back of a tablespoon, gently push the mixture down into the tin to get rid of any air pockets. Cover with clingfilm, directly on the surface of the cake, and freeze until solid (overnight is best).

**5.** Boil the reserved cherry liquid fast, until syrupy and reduced to around 2 tbsp. It will thicken up when it's cold. (If it's too thick when cold, loosen with a smidge of boiling water.)

**6.** Serve the cake straight from the freezer. Unmould onto a large platter. Remelt the reserved chocolate and drizzle from a teaspoon, zigzagging all over the cake and platter; repeat with some of the syrup. Pile fresh cherries in the middle, scatter with pistachios and dust with icing sugar. Cut with a large, sharp knife.

### Hints & Tips

If using tinned cherries, 1 tbsp of cherry brandy or Amaretto is a nice addition when reducing the syrup (step 5).

(V)

# RHUBARB & ELDERFLOWER FOOL WITH OAT CRUNCH

SERVES 6

500g (1lb 2oz) rhubarb
4 tbsp elderflower cordial
4 tbsp caster sugar
425ml (15fl oz) double cream

FOR THE OAT CRUNCH
a knob of butter
2 tbsp oats
1 tbsp demerara sugar

**You can't beat a fool for speed, ease and deliciousness. The oat crunch adds welcome texture and is irresistible with or without the fool!**

1. Preheat the oven to 190°C.

2. Wipe the rhubarb stems and cut into 3.5cm (1½in) chunks. Place in a shallow ovenproof dish large enough to take the rhubarb without piling it up too much, dribble over the elderflower cordial and scatter over the caster sugar. Bake in the preheated oven for 10–15 minutes or until the rhubarb is just cooked. The time will depend on the thickness of the stems.

3. Tip the rhubarb into a sieve suspended over a bowl and leave to drain until cold. Reserve the juice.

4. Whip the cream until it forms soft peaks – be careful not to overwhip it, as it will thicken further when you fold in the rhubarb.

5. Break the rhubarb up a little with a fork – I like to leave a few chunky textural bits, rather than make a purée, but purée it if you prefer, then fold gently and not too thoroughly into the cream, leaving a ripple effect. Spoon into pretty glasses, small dishes or one large bowl. Cover and refrigerate.

6. To make the oat crunch, melt the butter in a pan, add the oats and sugar and stir-fry until golden, caramelized and crunchy. Set aside to cool

7. Just before serving, spoon a little reserved juice over the fools and top with the oat crunch.

### Get Ahead

Complete step 2 up to 4 days in advance. Make to the end of step 5 up to 2 days in advance. The oat crunch lasts for several weeks in an airtight container.

### Hints & Tips

- 2 small pieces (or 1 large) of finely chopped stem ginger added to the rhubarb tastes delicious and rings the changes.
- The oat crunch is heavenly with just about anything – yoghurt, creamy puddings, panna cotta, porridge and ice cream, to name but a few.

# SEVILLE ORANGE POSSET WITH SEVILLE ORANGE SABLÉS

Ⓥ

SERVES 8

**4 Seville oranges**
**600ml (1 pint) double cream**
**150g (5½oz) caster sugar**
**Seville orange marmalade and orange zest, to decorate**

### Get Ahead

Make to the end of step 4 up to 2 days ahead.

**Puddings don't get much easier than this – three ingredients, three minutes' cooking and a sublime result!**

**1.** Using a fine grater, grate the zest from one orange and set aside for decoration. Squeeze the juice from all four oranges. Get ready 8 glasses, small china or glass pots, or pretty cups and saucers.

**2.** Put the cream and sugar in a pan (not non-stick) large enough for the cream to expand and bubble up during fast boiling. Stir occasionally until it comes to the boil, then boil rapidly for exactly 3 minutes.

**3.** Remove from the heat, whisk in the orange juice and pour into the glasses. Allow to cool, then cover and refrigerate for at least 4 hours, until set (overnight is best).

**4.** Decorate with a little Seville orange marmalade and the reserved orange zest.

## SEVILLE ORANGE SABLÉS

MAKES APPROXIMATELY 16

**85g (3oz) plain flour**
**55g (2oz) butter**
**30g (1oz) golden caster sugar, plus a little extra**
**zest of 1 Seville orange, plus ½ tsp freshly squeezed juice**
**1 egg yolk**

**1.** Preheat the oven to 180°C.

**2.** Process the flour and butter together until they resemble breadcrumbs. Add the sugar, orange zest and juice, and egg yolk. Process again briefly, just until a smooth dough has formed.

**3.** On a floured surface, roll the dough into a chunky sausage shape with your hands, roughly 2.5cm (1in) in diameter. Wrap tightly in clingfilm and chill for 1 hour.

**4.** Cut the dough into discs a little thicker than a £1 coin and place on a baking sheet. Bake for 10–14 minutes or until the sablés are just beginning to turn a pale golden colour around the edges. Cool on a wire rack.

### Get Ahead

The sablés can be made in advance and stored in an airtight container for several weeks, or frozen.

### Hints & Tips

If making at the same time as the Seville Orange Posset, use the zest from one of the posset oranges before squeezing it, plus one teaspoon of its juice, for the biscuits (thus requiring one less orange).

# HAZELNUT MERINGUE & PRALINE TORTE

(V)

SERVES 16–20

**225g (8oz) hazelnuts, blanched**
**6 egg whites**
**a pinch of salt**
**340g (12oz) caster sugar**
**½ tsp vanilla extract**
**½ tsp white wine vinegar**
**100g (3½oz) granulated sugar**
**30g (1oz) dark chocolate**
**600ml (1 pint) double cream**

TO SERVE

**Cape gooseberries (physalis), pomegranate seeds, fresh berries, pouring cream (optional)**

### Get Ahead

- The meringues can be made several weeks ahead and stored in an airtight container or tightly wrapped in clingfilm, or frozen. The praline and shards can be made weeks ahead and stored in an airtight container, or frozen. The cream can be whipped at any time on the day and stored, covered, in the fridge, but underwhip it, as it will thicken while waiting.
- The torte can be finished off completely up to 4 hours in advance and it will still be crisp the next day.

### Hints & Tips

Don't worry if a few cracks appear – they add to the character! Fresh seasonal berries are lovely added to either of the layers, or serve a fruit compote separately.

**As well as looking impressive, this showstopping, graduated tower of layered meringue is ideal for entertaining large numbers, not least because it can be assembled hours in advance and slices like a dream!**

1. Preheat the oven to 150°C. Line 3 baking sheets with silicone paper or foil.

2. Toast 150g (5½oz) of the hazelnuts in a small dry frying pan until golden. Be careful, as they burn easily. Process (or grind, or crush with a pestle and mortar) until fairly fine. Let cool. Don't wash the processor or frying pan, as you will need them later for the praline.

3. Whisk the egg whites with a pinch of salt until stiff, then add the caster sugar a tablespoon at a time, whisking well between each addition. Add the vanilla extract and vinegar, and continue whisking until very stiff. Fold in the nuts using a large metal spoon.

4. Divide the mixture between the 3 baking sheets, with slightly more on one, a little less on the next and a little less still on the last one. Spread the larger amount evenly into a circle roughly 25cm (10 in) across, the next one a little smaller and the last one a little smaller again. Bake for 1 hour until crisp and dry. You may need to do this in 2 batches, depending on oven space.

5. Meanwhile, for the praline, lightly oil or line a baking sheet with silicone or baking paper. In the frying pan, gently heat the remaining hazelnuts with the granulated sugar, until the sugar has dissolved. Turn up the heat and bubble until caramelized and deep golden brown. Try not to stir once the sugar has melted. Quickly pour out onto the baking sheet in a thin layer. When cold, snap off a third of the brittle and grind this into praline the texture of granulated sugar. Snap or crack the remaining brittle into jagged shards. When ready to assemble, melt the chocolate in a small bowl suspended over a pan of boiling water. Whip the cream, *being careful not to overwhip. It should only just hold its shape.*

6. Put the largest meringue disc onto a flat serving plate or cake stand and carefully spread it with half the cream. Sit the medium-sized disc on top. *Gently* fold 3 heaped tablespoons of the praline into the cream. Just folding in the praline will thicken the cream even more – so beware! Spread over the second disc.

7. Top with the smallest disc. Dribble the melted chocolate in stripes over the top and down the sides using a teaspoon. Refrigerate until required. Just before serving, scatter with the remaining praline, and decorate with the shards and/or fruit, if using.

# INDIVIDUAL BLACKBERRY & APPLE OAT CRUMBLES

(V)

MAKES 8

**30g (1oz) butter**
**900g (2lb) cooking apples, peeled, cored and sliced**
**110g (4oz) caster sugar**
**½ tsp ground cinnamon**
**350g (12oz) blackberries**

FOR THE OAT CRUMBLE

**110g (4oz) plain flour**
**85g (3oz) butter**
**85g (3oz) demerara sugar**
**55g (2oz) rolled oats**

### Get Ahead

Make entirely up to 3 days in advance, cover and refrigerate, or freeze, but don't cook until required.

**Everyone loves a crumble and, for entertaining, this humble but delicious pudding looks considerably more elegant when cooked individually – less Sunday lunch or nursery pudding! The fact they can be made days in advance or frozen adds to their charm. They thaw out very quickly and so are useful to have in the freezer for when a quick pudding is required or a busy weekend necessitates some advance preparation.**

**1.** Melt the butter in a saucepan, add the apples, caster sugar and cinnamon, and cook gently until the apples begin to soften into a purée. Add the blackberries and cook for a few minutes longer. There should be a few chunky bits of apple remaining. Taste and add more sugar if necessary. Spoon into 8 individual ovenproof dishes or ramekins.

**2.** Preheat the oven to 190°C.

**3.** Put all the crumble ingredients, except the oats, into a processor and whizz until the mixture resembles breadcrumbs (or rub the flour and butter together by hand). Add the oats and stir in, or give them a very quick whizz so as not to break them up.

**4.** Pile on top of the apple mixture and cook in the preheated oven for 15–20 minutes or until golden brown and bubbling.

### Hints & Tips

- I like a high crumble-to-fruit ratio, so this quantity is generous – just pile it high! If you prefer less, any that's leftover will freeze beautifully. It's a good idea to make a double quantity of crumble mixture and freeze what you don't need, then you've got some spare for a speedy crumble. It doesn't freeze solid, so it's easily scattered by the spoonful straight from the freezer.
- There are endless possibilities for the base, such as plums, gooseberries with elderflower, and rhubarb and ginger.

# PEAR & FRANGIPANE TART



(V)

SERVES 12

2 x 400g (14oz) tins of pear halves in syrup, drained
caster sugar, for sprinkling (optional)
icing sugar, for dusting

FOR THE PASTRY
225g (8oz) plain flour, plus extra for kneading
110g (4oz) butter, diced
110g (4oz) caster sugar
3 egg yolks
1 tbsp cold water

FOR THE FRANGIPANE
170g (6oz) butter, softened
170g (6oz) caster sugar
170g (6oz) ground almonds
3 eggs
2 tbsp plain flour

TO SERVE
Crème fraîche or double cream

### Get Ahead

Make up to 3 days in advance and keep, covered, in the fridge, or freeze.

**This lovely tart is considerably easier to make than it looks, largely because all the work is done in a processor. It is also a bit of a cheat, using tinned pears instead of fresh. Very good for entertaining and your guests might even mistake you for an award-winning pâtissier!**

1. Put all the pastry ingredients into a food processor and process gently using the pulse button if you have one, until everything just begins to come together into a crumbly ball. Remove and knead lightly, using a little extra flour until it has formed a smoothish ball. Wrap in clingfilm and chill in the fridge for 30 minutes.

2. Preheat the oven to 190°C.

3. Meanwhile, make the frangipane. Using the unwashed processor bowl, process all the frangipane ingredients together until a smooth paste has formed. Don't worry if it curdles. Set aside.

4. Between 2 sheets of clingfilm, roll out the pastry as best you can – it will be very short and crumbly – and line a 28cm (11in) loose-bottomed tart tin. The pastry may fall apart but it is very malleable and you can just mould and push it into the tin using your fingers; treat it gently and don't overwork it, though.

5. Spoon the frangipane into the bottom of the pastry case and smooth the surface.

6. Dry the pears on kitchen paper. Cut into slices widthways, slide onto a palette knife and press down on them so that the slices fan out into a sliced pear shape. Arrange them on top of the frangipane in a circle. Slide the tin onto a baking sheet.

7. Bake in the preheated oven for 40 minutes or until the pastry is golden and the filling is just set. If necessary, turn the oven up to 220°C, sprinkle with a little extra caster sugar and cook for 10–15 minutes or until golden brown. Leave to cool in the tin for 15 minutes, then remove from the tin and cool on a wire rack. Serve warm, or at room temperature, dusted with icing sugar and with crème fraîche or double cream.

### Hints & Tips

- If you prefer a caramelized finish to the tart, give the top the once-over with a cook's blowtorch. Or for a shiny finish, glaze with apricot jam – melt a little apricot glaze or jam with a dribble of water and brush all over the top of the tart, making sure the entire surface is glazed.
- Apricots make a lovely alternative. You will need about 14 fresh apricots, stoned. I like to arrange the outer circle of apricots cut-side down and the inner circle cut-side up, with a star anise in each cavity.

## A



## B



## C

## D

## M



## N



## O



## P

## ACKNOWLEDGEMENTS

I have so enjoyed writing this book. Developing and writing recipes is almost an addiction for me. Even when short of time, I can't stop myself from turning whatever ingredients are to hand into a new recipe. Therefore, I am so grateful to the kind, and in many cases loyal, people who come to my demonstrations around the country, for affording me the opportunity to share some of these recipes. Heartfelt thanks to you all for your encouragement, support and feedback about recipes you've cooked, which I love receiving. I am thrilled to have another opportunity, through this book, to share more of these recipes with a wider audience.

The demonstrations are immeasurably enhanced by my oldest, dearest friend and helper, Sally Politmore, whose support and kindness know no bounds. Thank you, Sal, for your characteristic and never-ending good humour and for making it all such fun – we've certainly had some escapades! Also, big thanks to all the kind people who generously offer their kitchens to us and put up with our invasions with such geniality and tolerance.

I have so many talented people to thank for their expertise and invaluable insight and whose contributions make *The Get-Ahead Cook* into the beautiful book that it is. I would like to give particular thanks to John Bond and Annabel Wright from Whitefox, for being so encouraging, supportive and efficient. Also to delightful project editor Zia Mattocks, who has overseen and held everything together beautifully and coped calmly and sympathetically with my shortcomings. Thank you so much, Zia! Thanks to copy editor Gillian Haslam, for spotting and righting my mistakes, and to talented Louise Evans, for her wonderful, clear layout and design.

To Tony Briscoe, photographer extraordinaire, who gamely travelled from London to deepest Northumberland to shoot the photographs on location. Not only are your photographs wonderful, Tony, but also your eye for detail and styling, combined with bags of patience. What fun it was! The recipes are greatly enhanced by prop stylist Hannah Wilkinson's excellent vision and inspired interpretation of them – I just wish I could have kept the props! We could not have managed the shoots without the tireless help, support, eagle eye and input of my youngest daughter Lucy, who kept us on schedule, cooked, hand-modelled and was generally responsible for the smooth running of each day. We were ably assisted by Tora Joicey, who kept us clean and tidy, and always with a smile. Thank you both.

My friend Amanda Finley, who has kindly been testing my recipes for years. I value her feedback enormously; she is meticulous and her observations have improved many of these recipes. Thank you, Amanda, and also Gillian Millar, for the recipes you have so kindly tested in the build-up.

I owe very big thanks to Karen Miller, who always keeps my life straight in the office, for so proficiently looking after the demonstrations and shop while I've been focusing on the book.

To my marvellous and wise agent Heather Holden-Brown, who is reassuring, funny and kind, and always has my best interests at heart. Heather, thank you so much for everything, not least our lively early morning calls!

And the biggest thanks of all go to my wonderful family, Flora, Freddie, Lucy and John, who are always so supportive and encouraging of everything I do – and uncomplainingly put up with endless recipe testing! My long-suffering husband John's advice and encouragement are invaluable. He takes all my trials and tribulations in his stride, not to mention sometimes eating food that he only 'quite' likes, and frequently over and over again in my bid get a recipe right. And, to add insult to injury, he often has to wait for it to be photographed before he can eat it!

## ABOUT THE AUTHOR

Jane Lovett is an experienced cook who runs popular cookery demonstrations around the UK. Having obtained a diploma at Le Cordon Bleu, London, she has taught at Leiths School of Food and Wine, contributed to and produced recipes and food for cookery books and magazines as a food stylist, and run her own successful London catering business providing imaginative food for high-profile clients.

Jane lives with her husband, John, in rural North Northumberland, where she relishes country life. A keen gardener, she enjoys growing and cooking her own fruit and vegetables, which are the starting point of many of her seasonal recipes. She writes a monthly column for *The Northumbrian Magazine* as well as contributing to other publications. Jane is a regular demonstrator at Divertimenti in London and the author of *Make it Easy* (2015).

www.janelovett.com